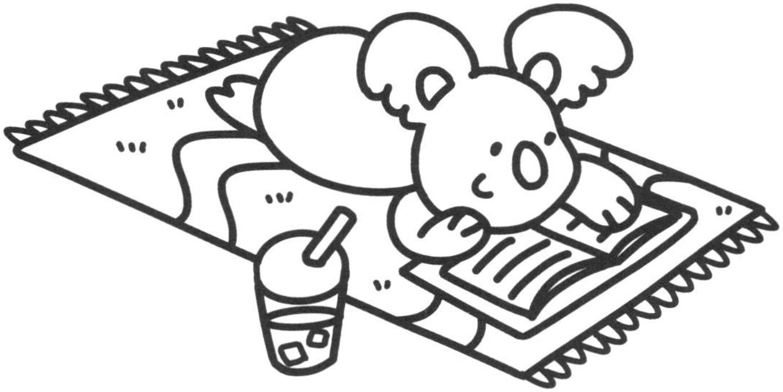

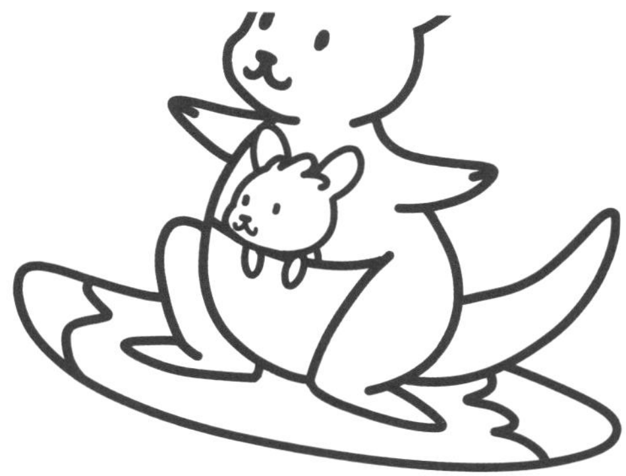

This book belongs to:

....

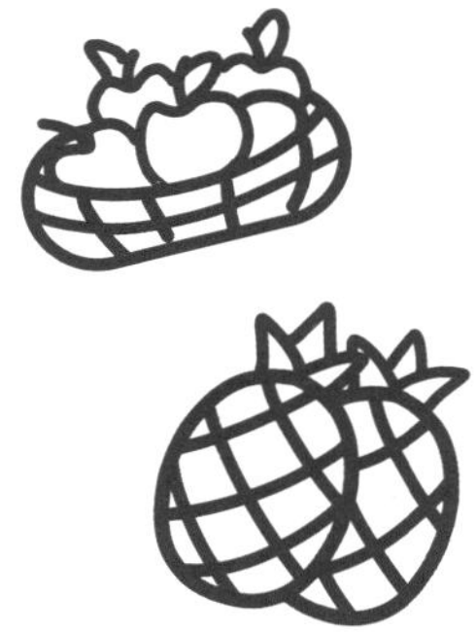

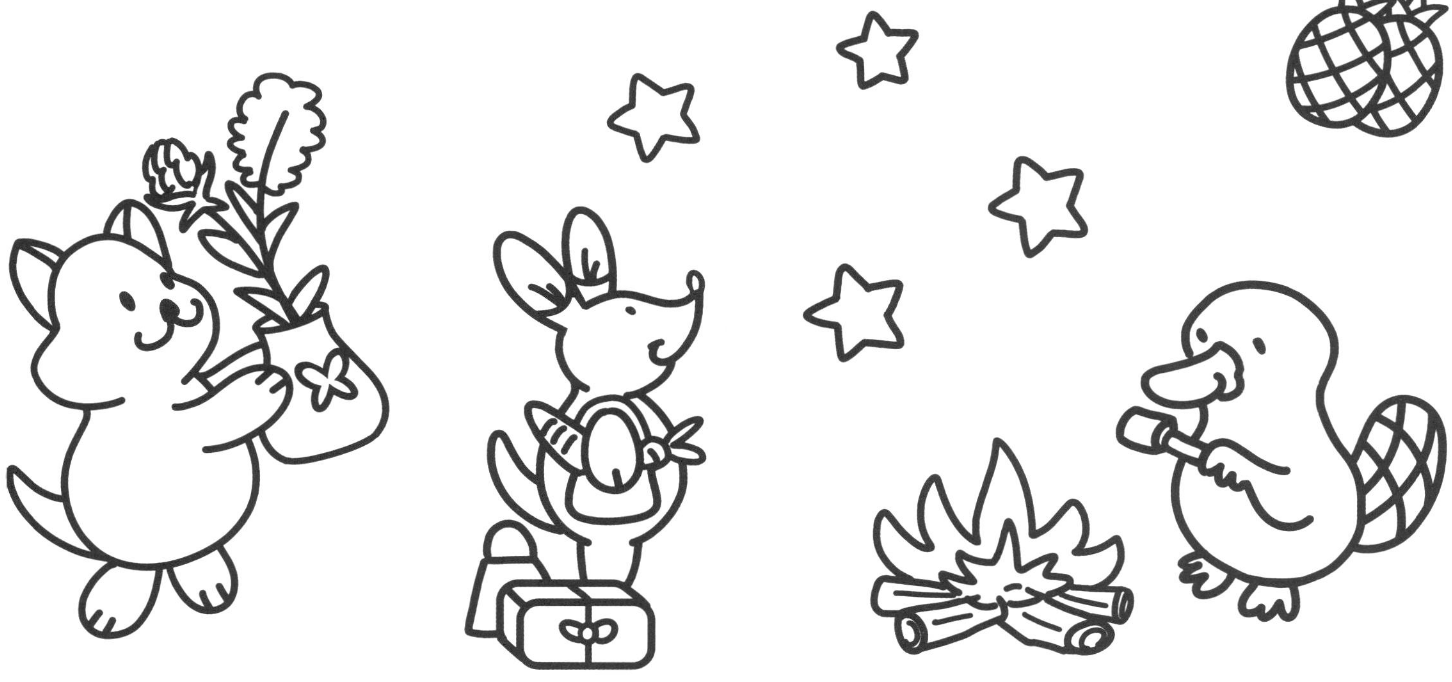

First published by Albert Street Books, an imprint of Allen & Unwin, in 2025

Allen & Unwin
Cammeraygal Country
83 Alexander Street
Crows Nest NSW 2065
Australia
Phone: (61 2) 8425 0100
Email: info@allenandunwin.com
Web: www.allenandunwin.com

Allen & Unwin acknowledges the Traditional Owners of the Country on which we live and work. We pay our respects to all Aboriginal and Torres Strait Islander Elders, past and present.

EU Authorised Representative: Easy Access System Europe,
Mustamäe tee 50, 10621 Tallinn, Estonia, gpsr.requests@easproject.com

NATIONAL LIBRARY OF AUSTRALIA
A catalogue record for this book is available from the National Library of Australia

ISBN 978 1 76118 250 1

For teaching resources, explore allenandunwin.com/learn

Cover and text design by Hana Kinoshita Thomson
Set in 16 pt Noyh R Regular by Hana Kinoshita Thomson
Printed and bound in Australia by the Opus Group

10 9 8 7 6 5 4 3 2 1

FSC www.fsc.org MIX Paper | Supporting responsible forestry FSC® C001695

HELLO SUNSHINE

cosy Aussie colouring

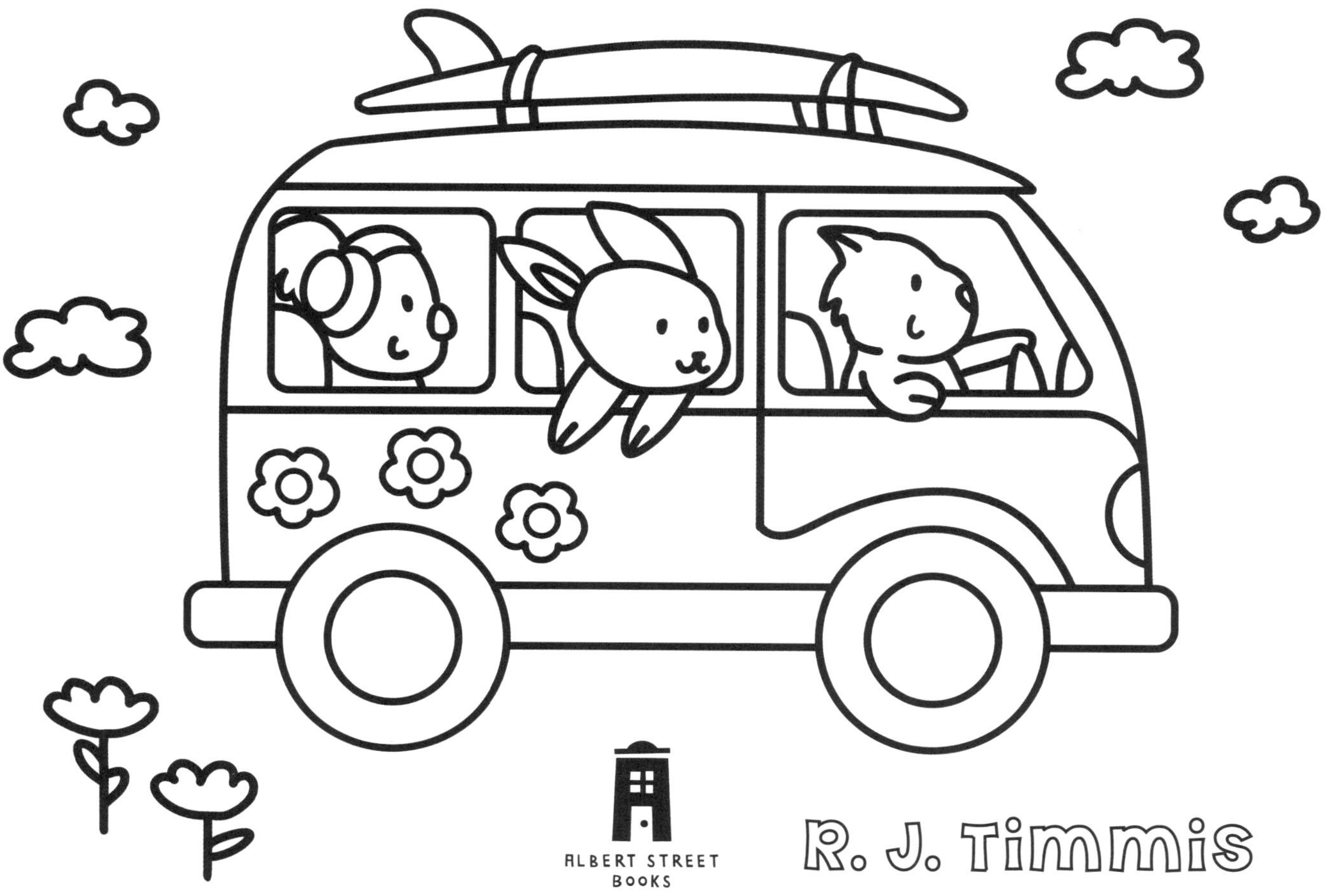

ALBERT STREET BOOKS

R. J. Timmis

HELLO, FRIEND!

Colouring is a great way to slow down, clear your mind and enjoy a little creative me-time. So, find a comfy spot, grab your favourite colouring tools and let the fun begin!

BEFORE YOU START

You can use the very first page of this book to test your markers, colour pencils or crayons.

Don't forget to place a piece of card or thick paper behind the page you're working on to protect the next illustration.

HAPPY COLOURING!

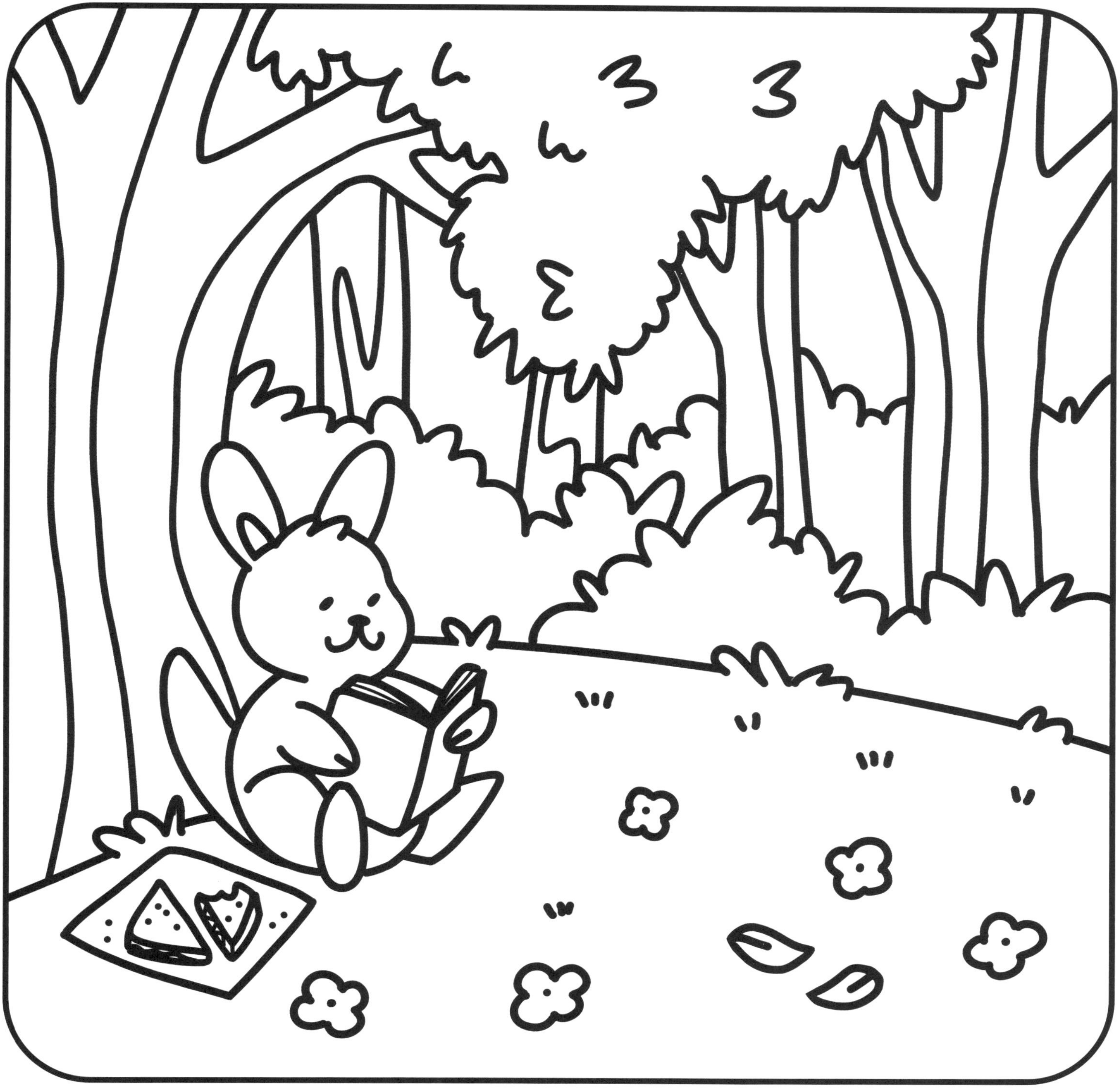

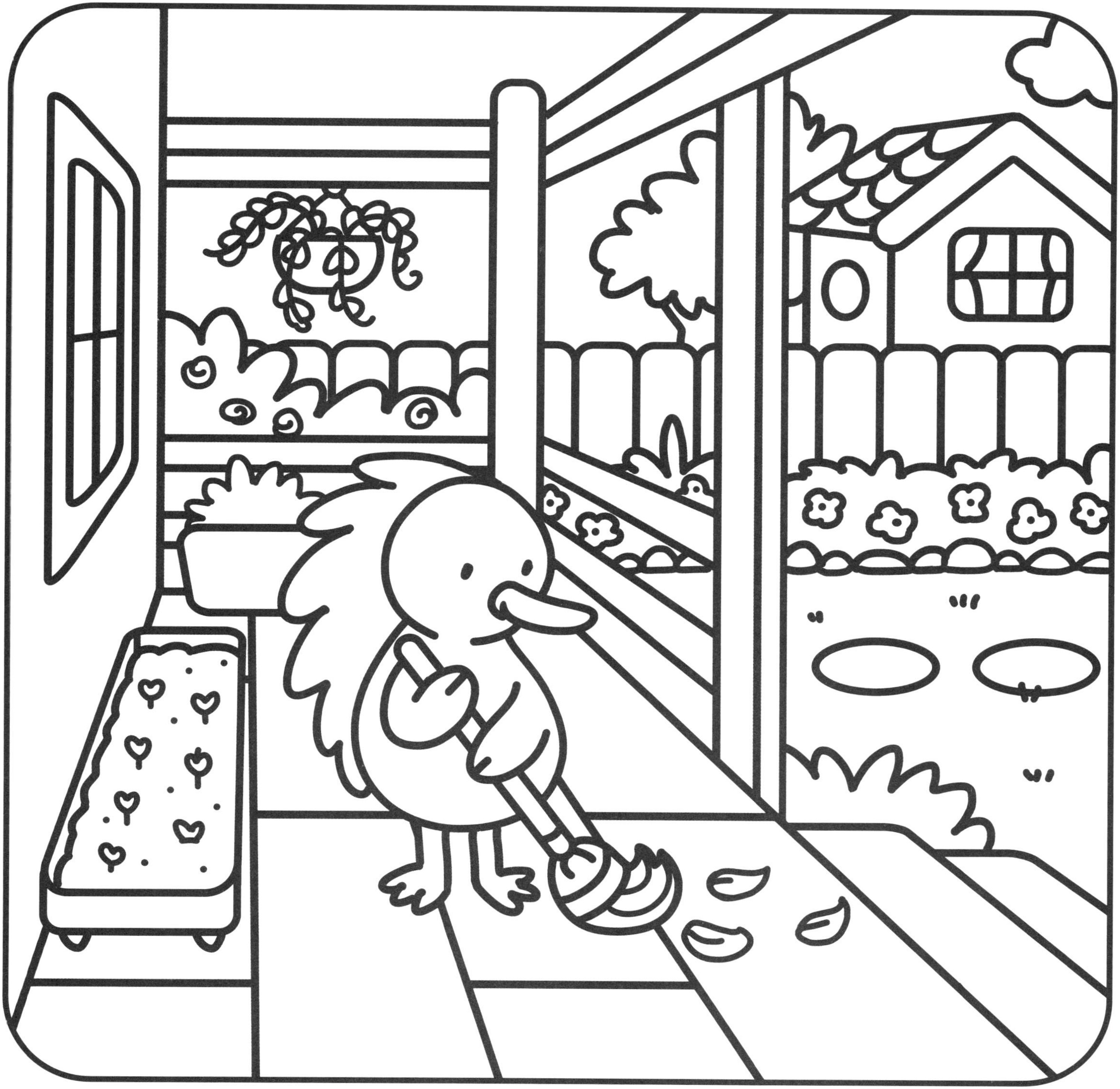

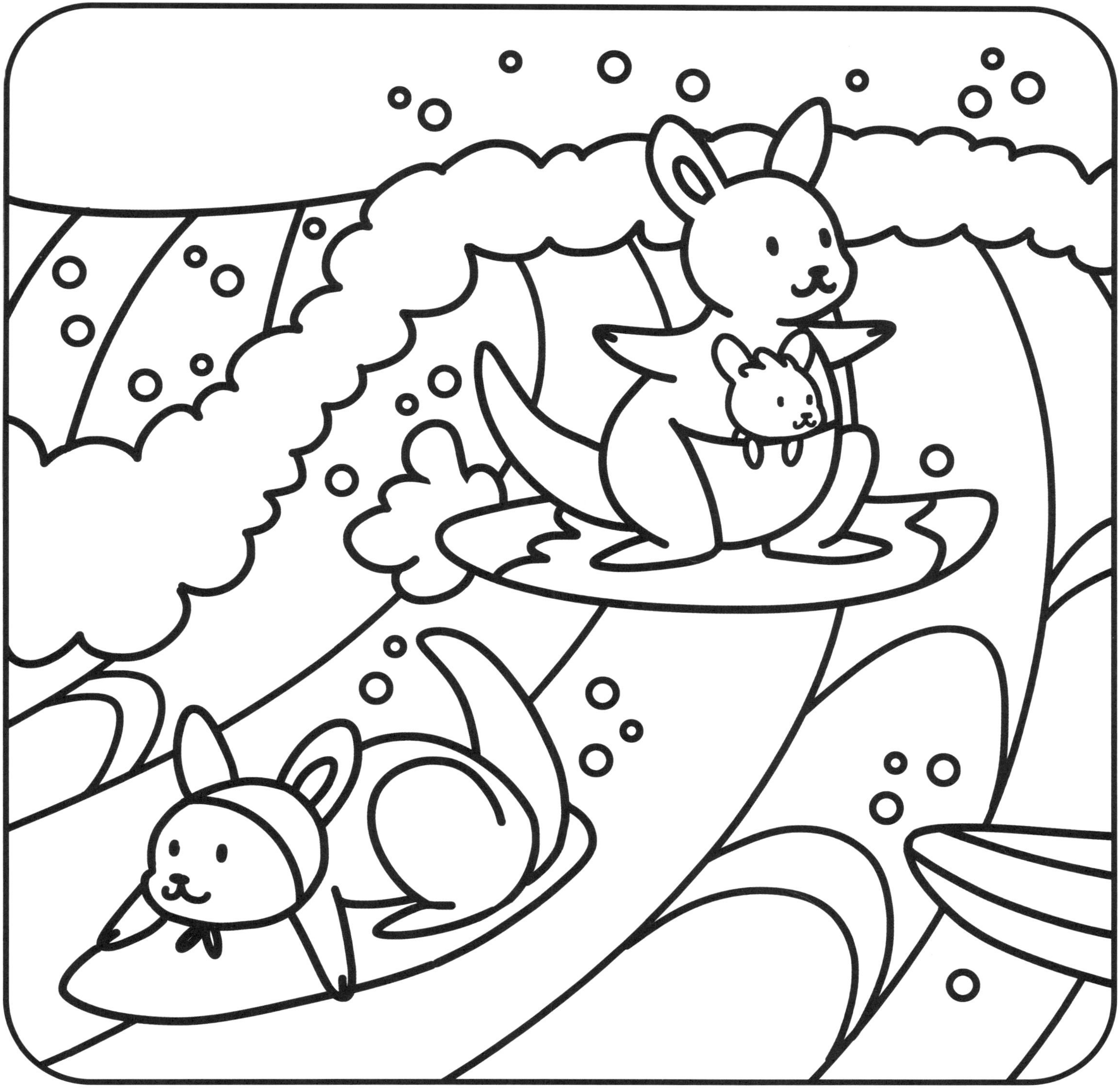

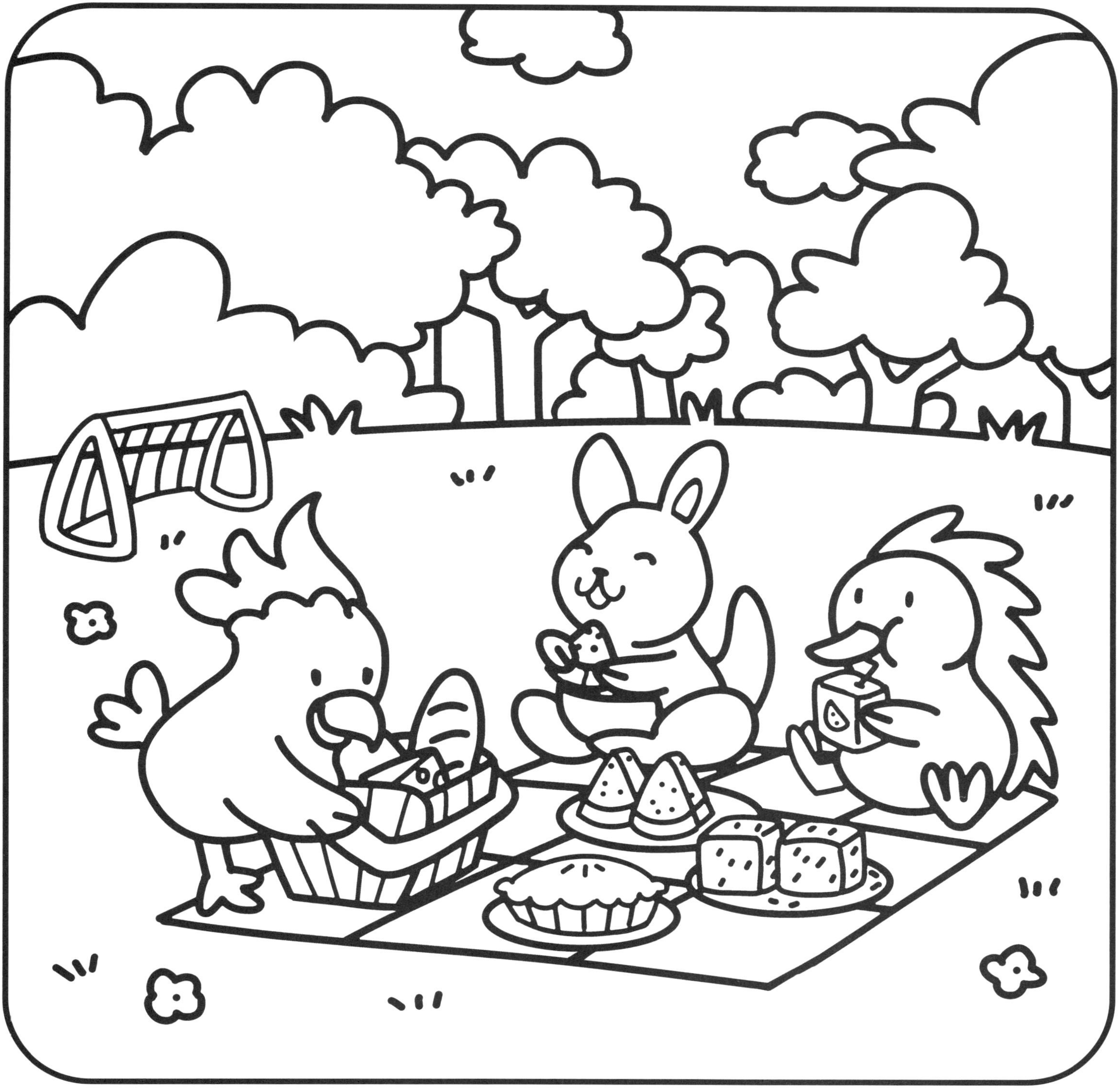

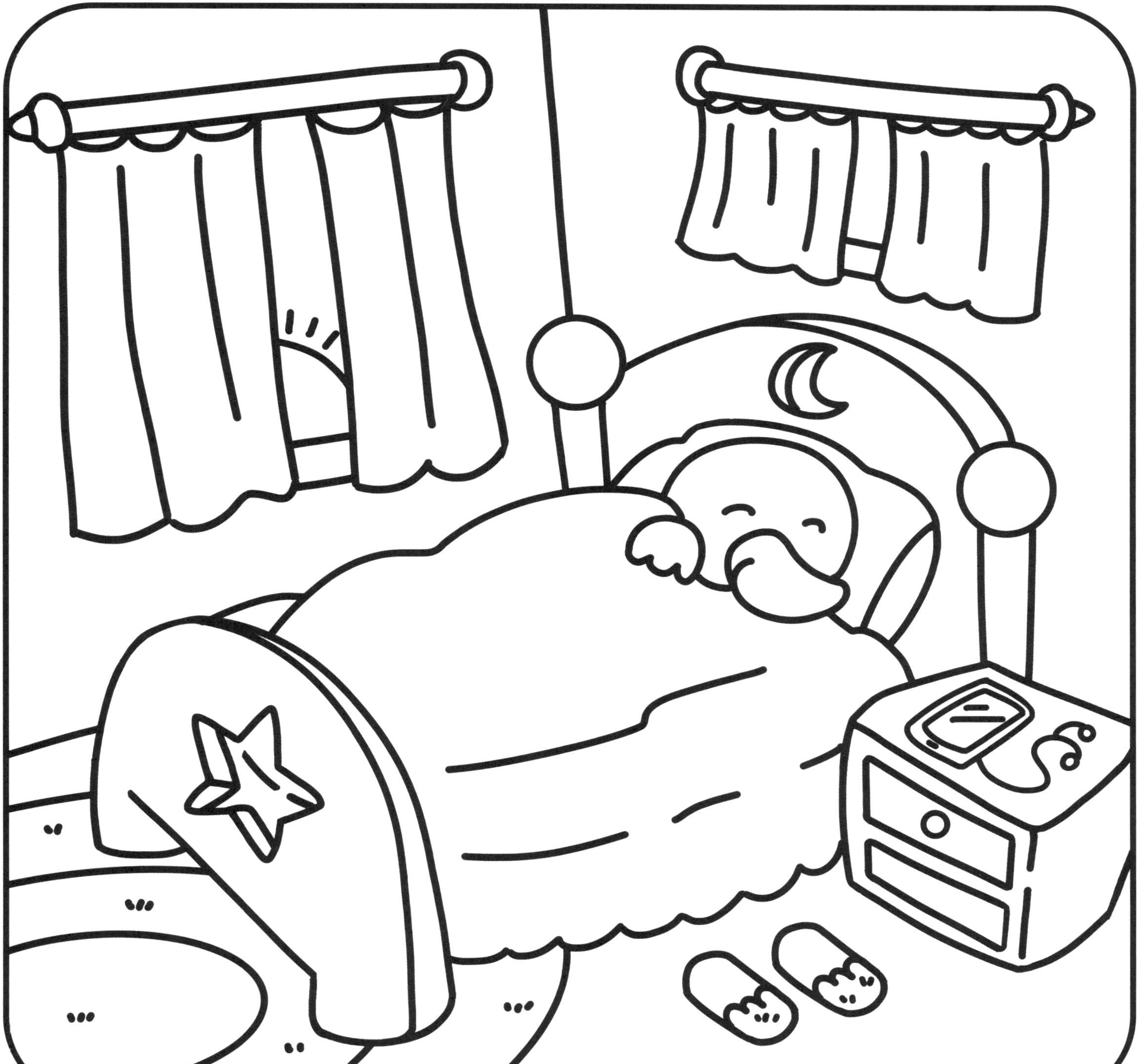

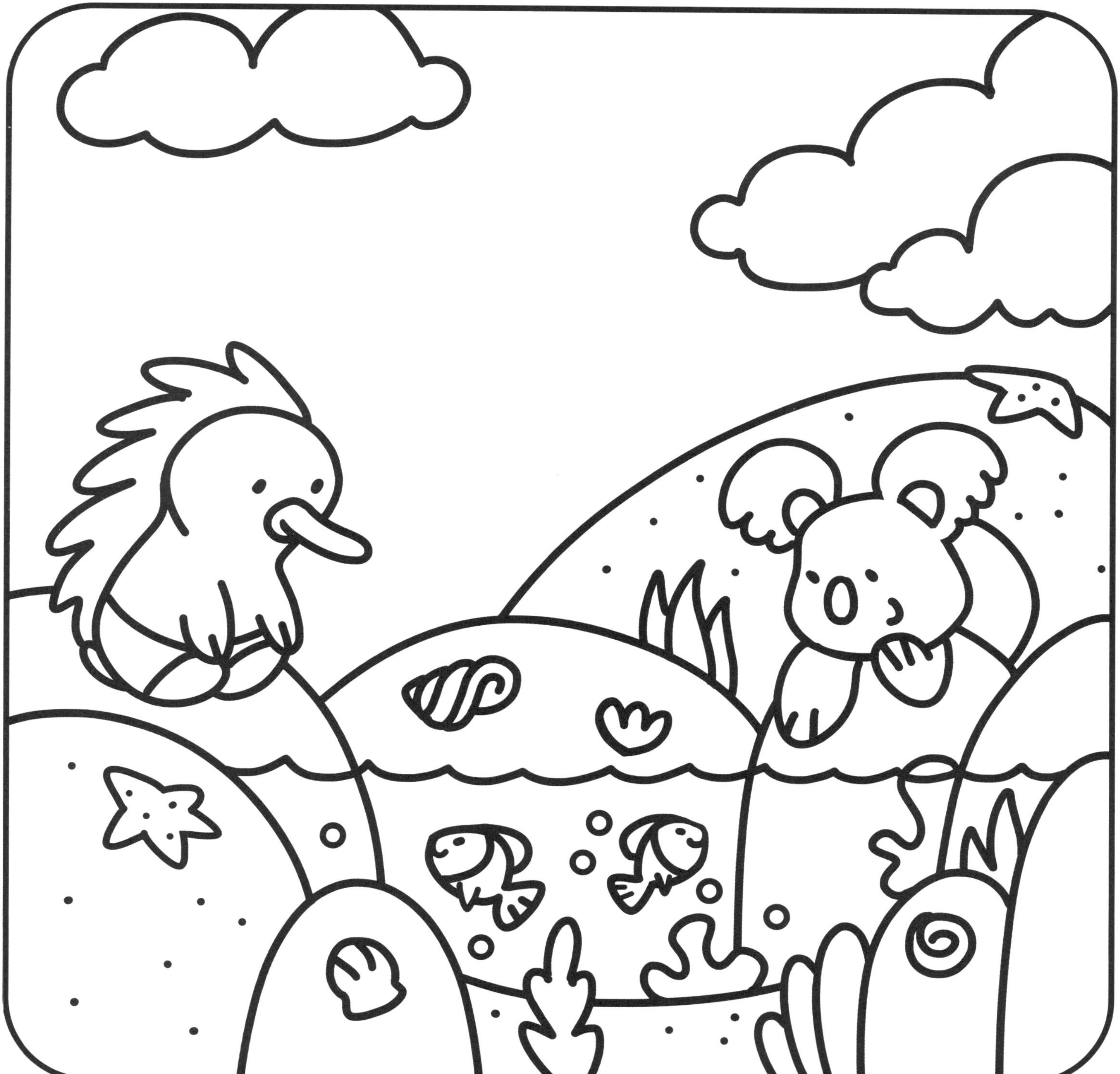

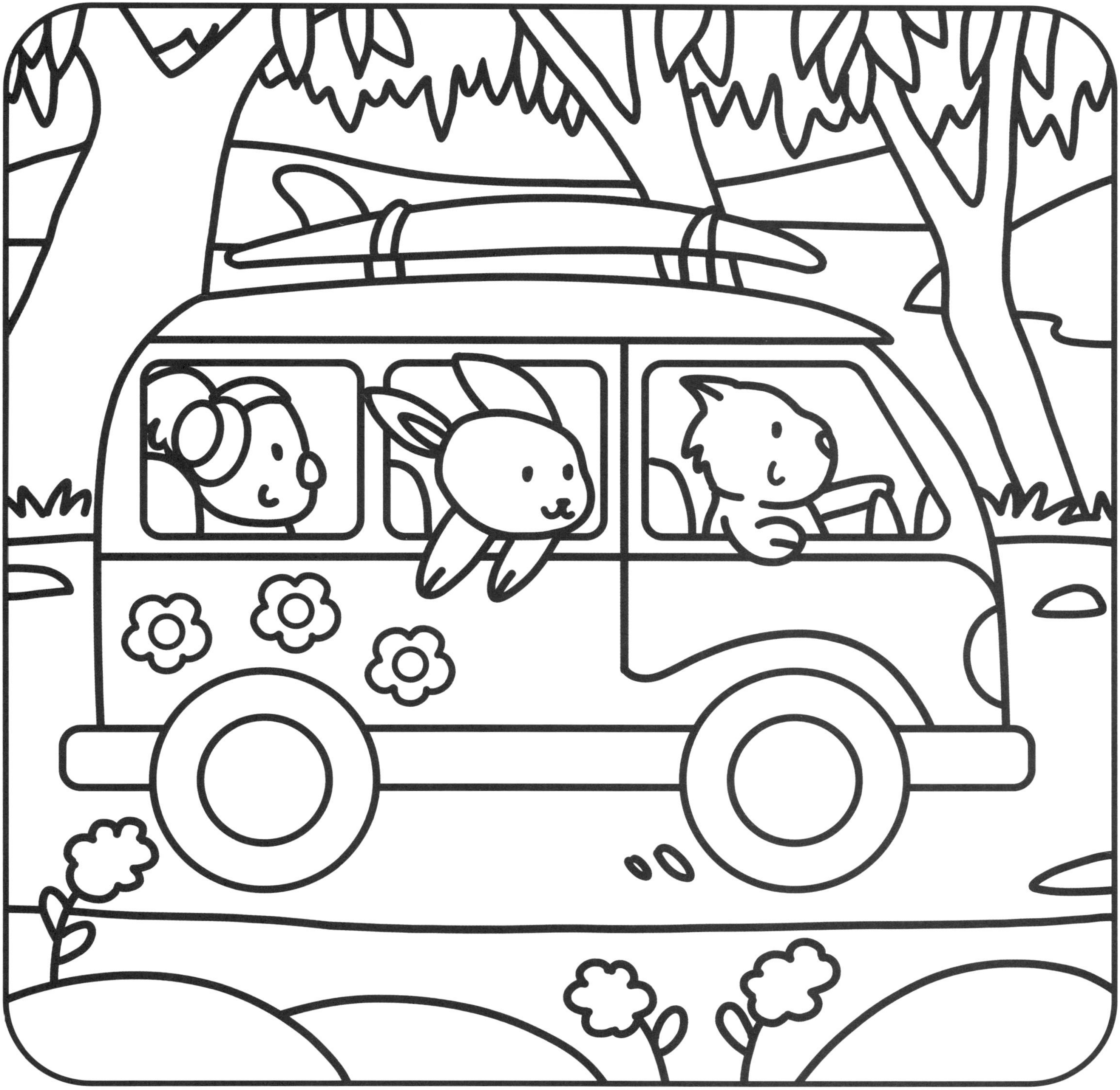

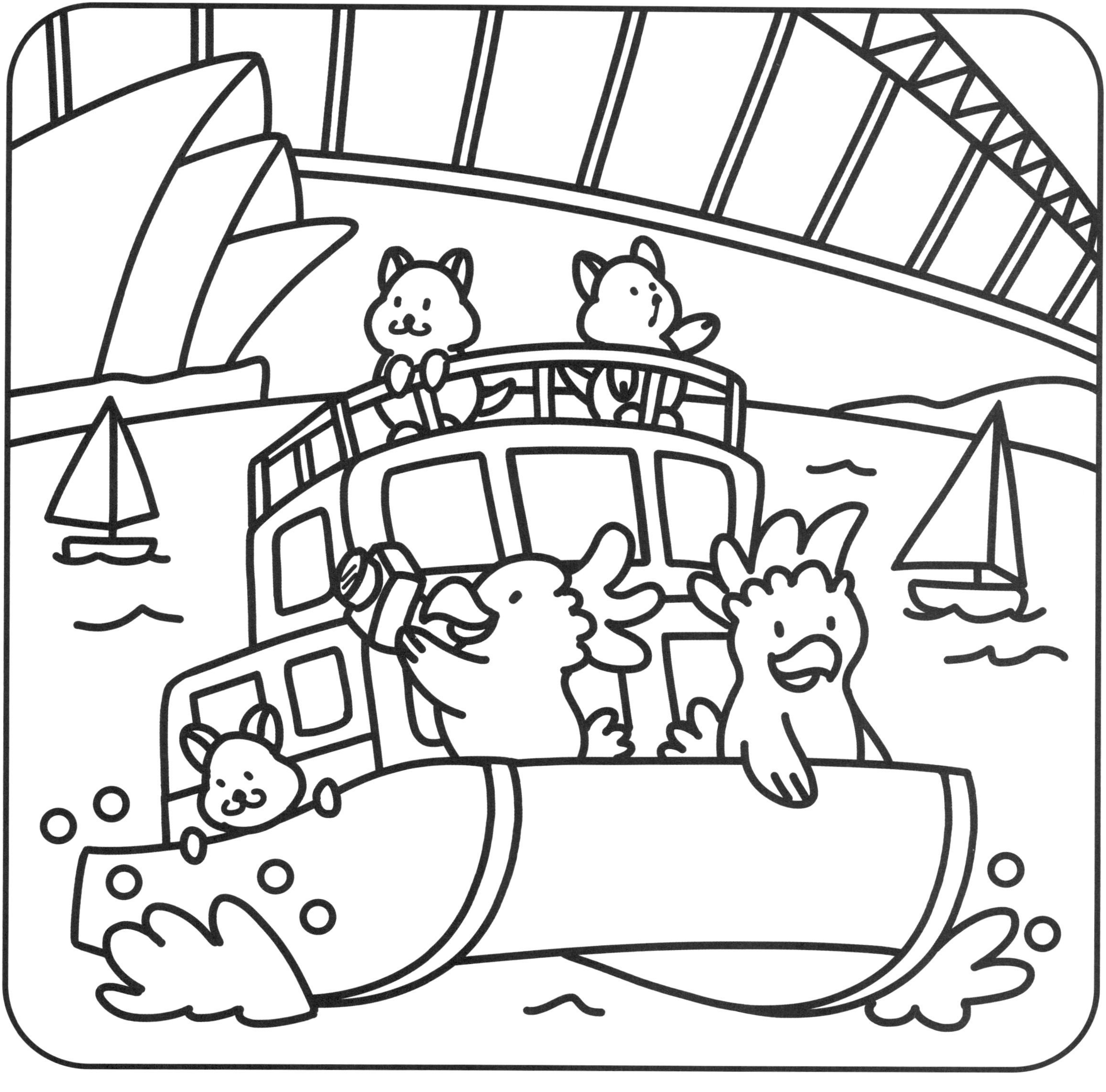

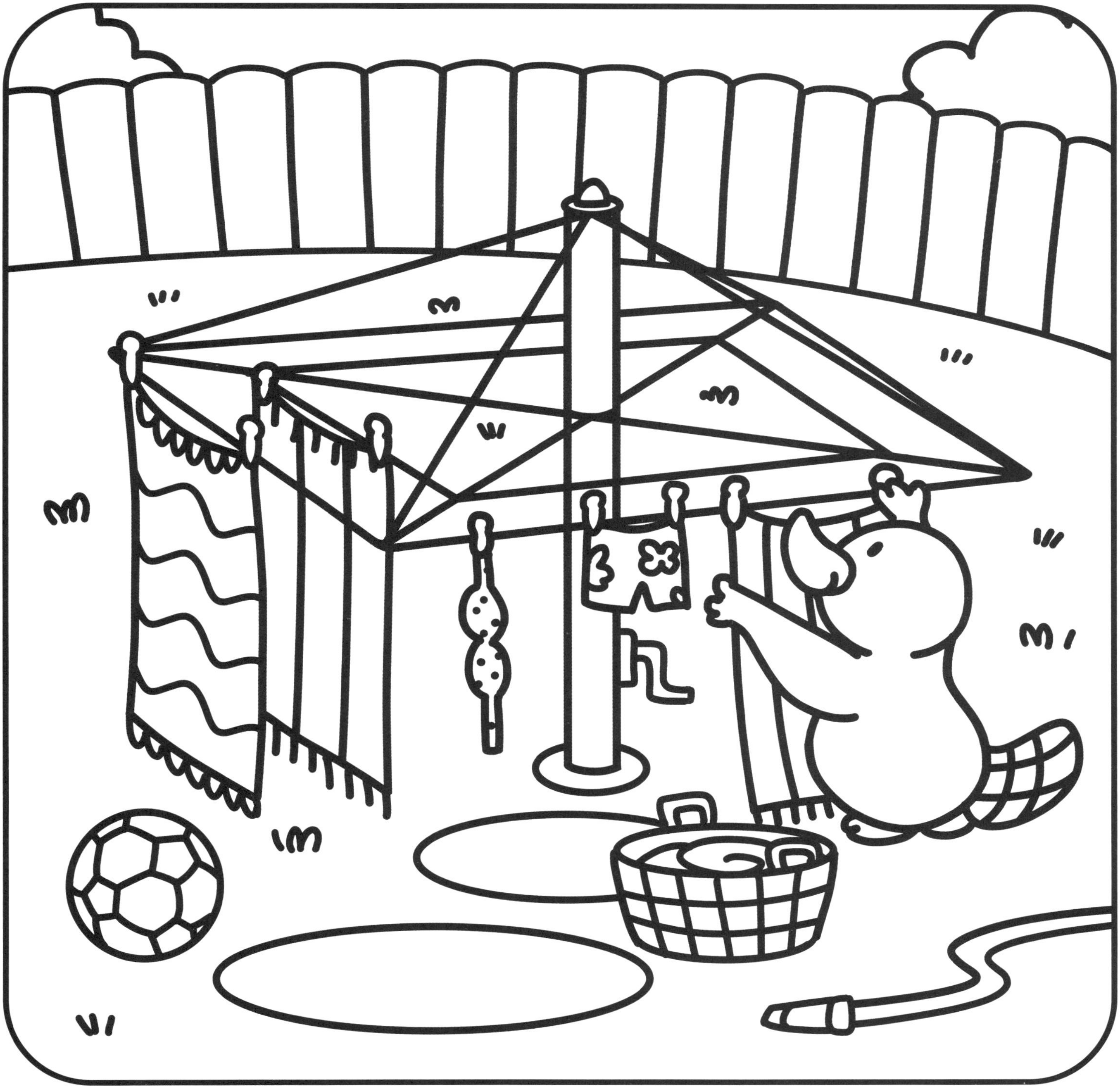

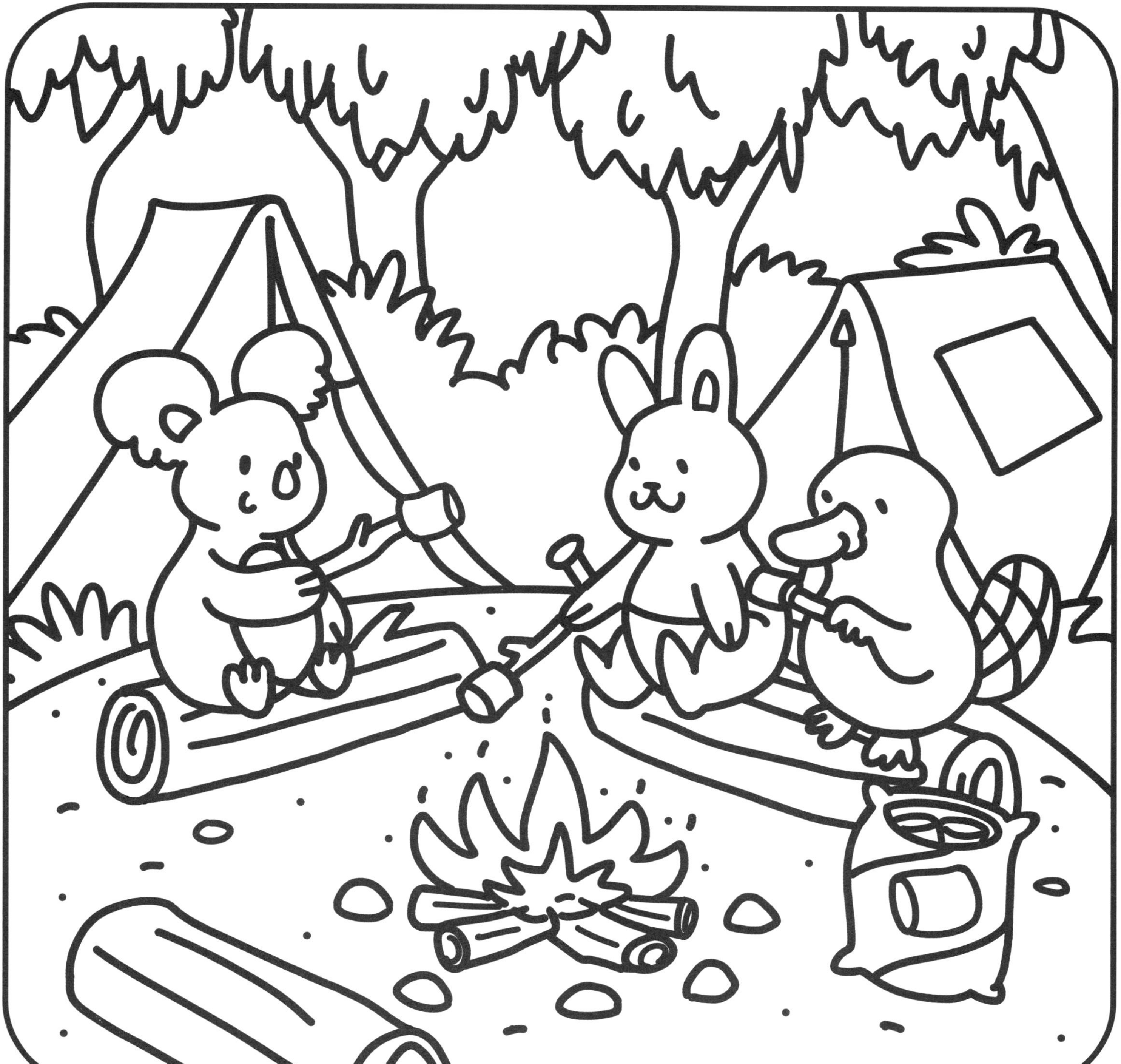

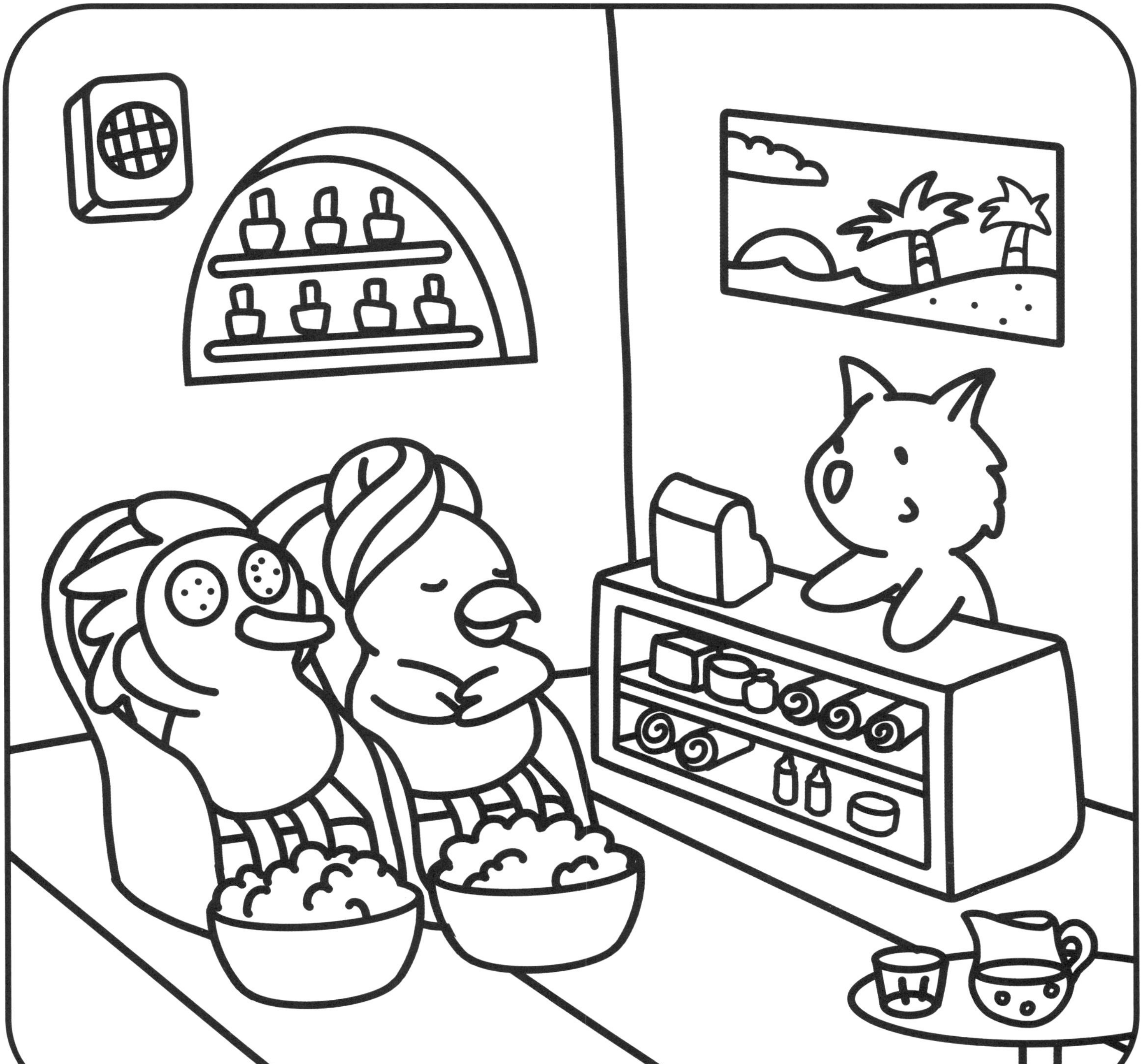

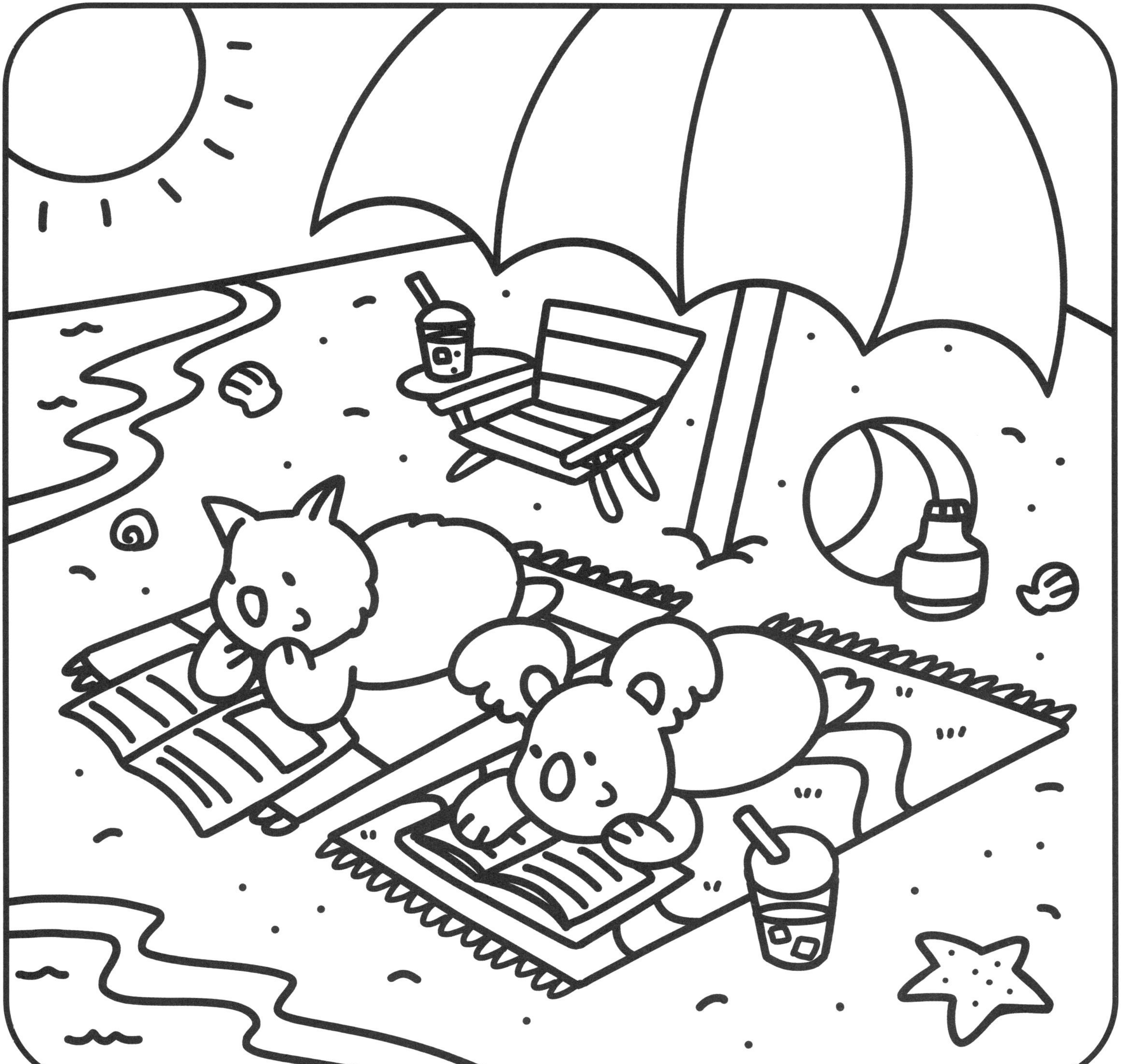

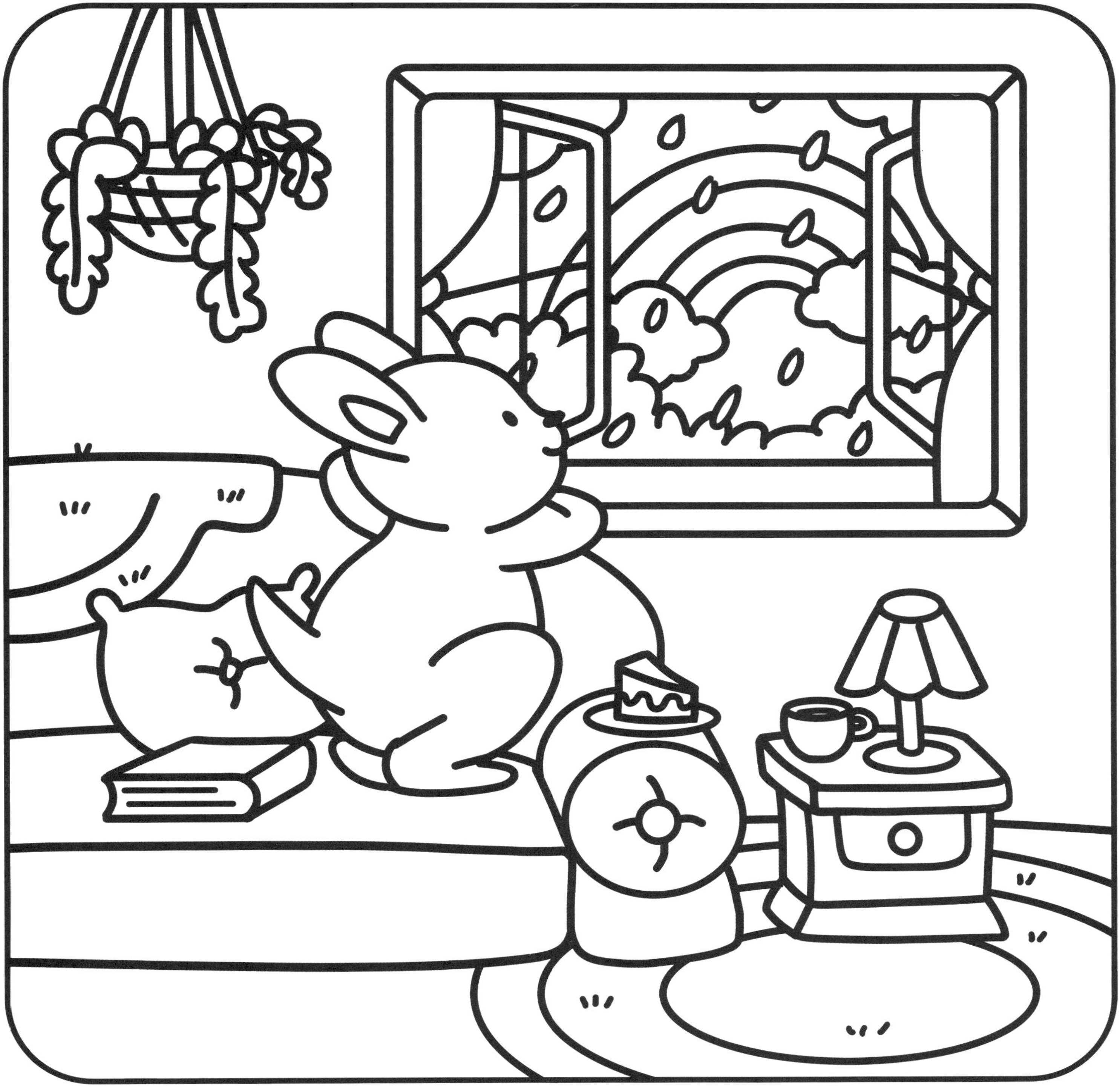

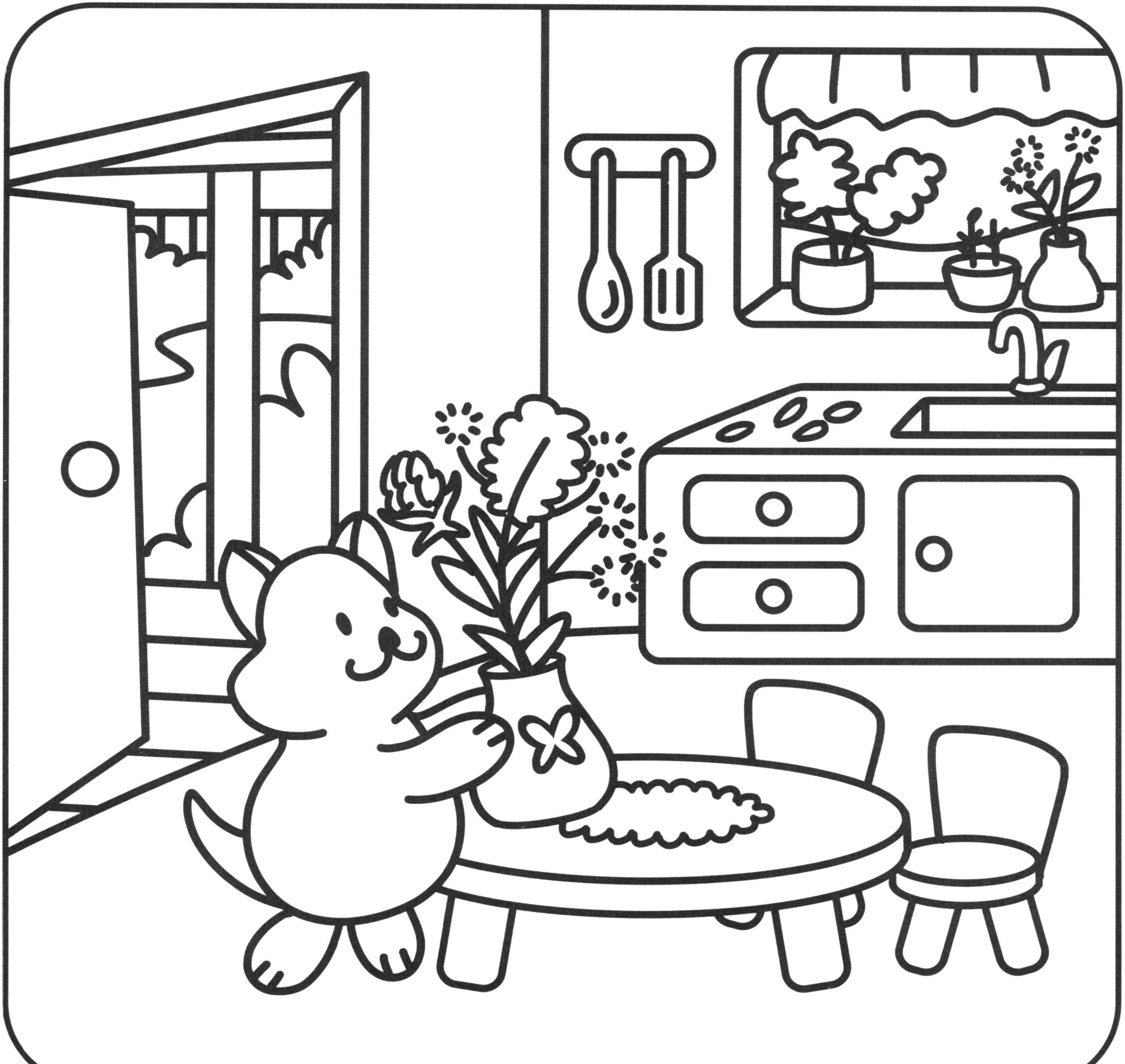

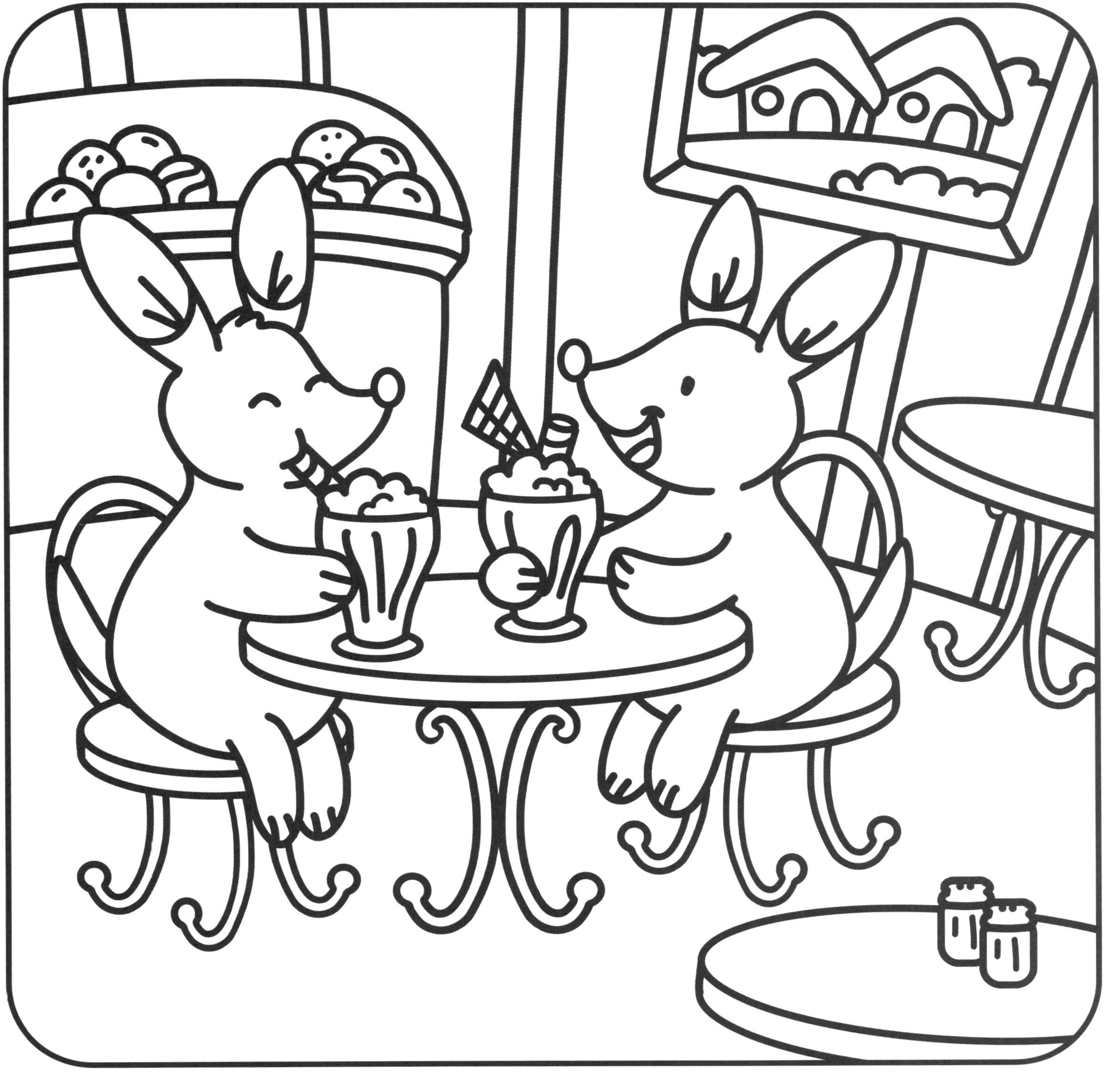

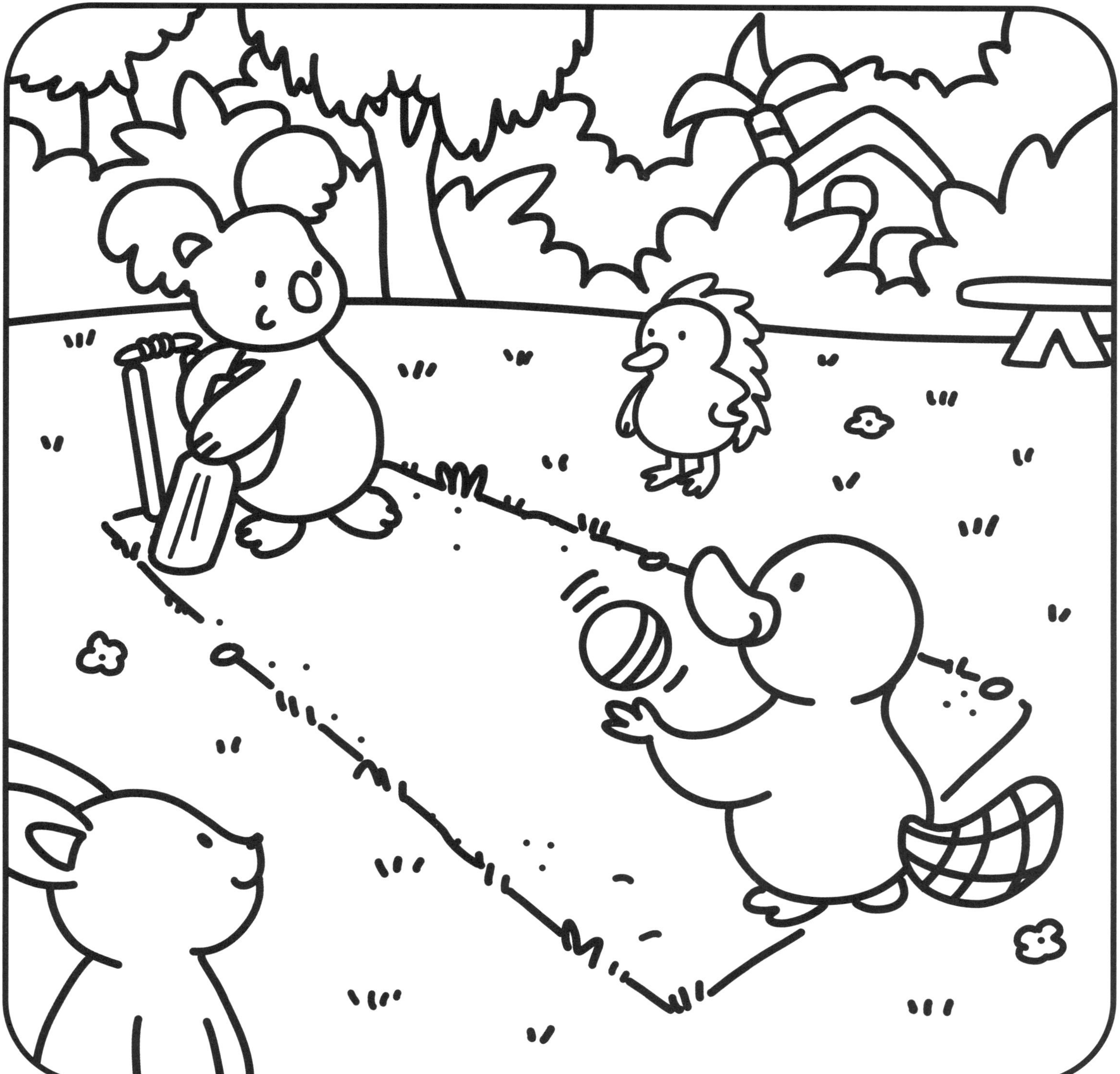

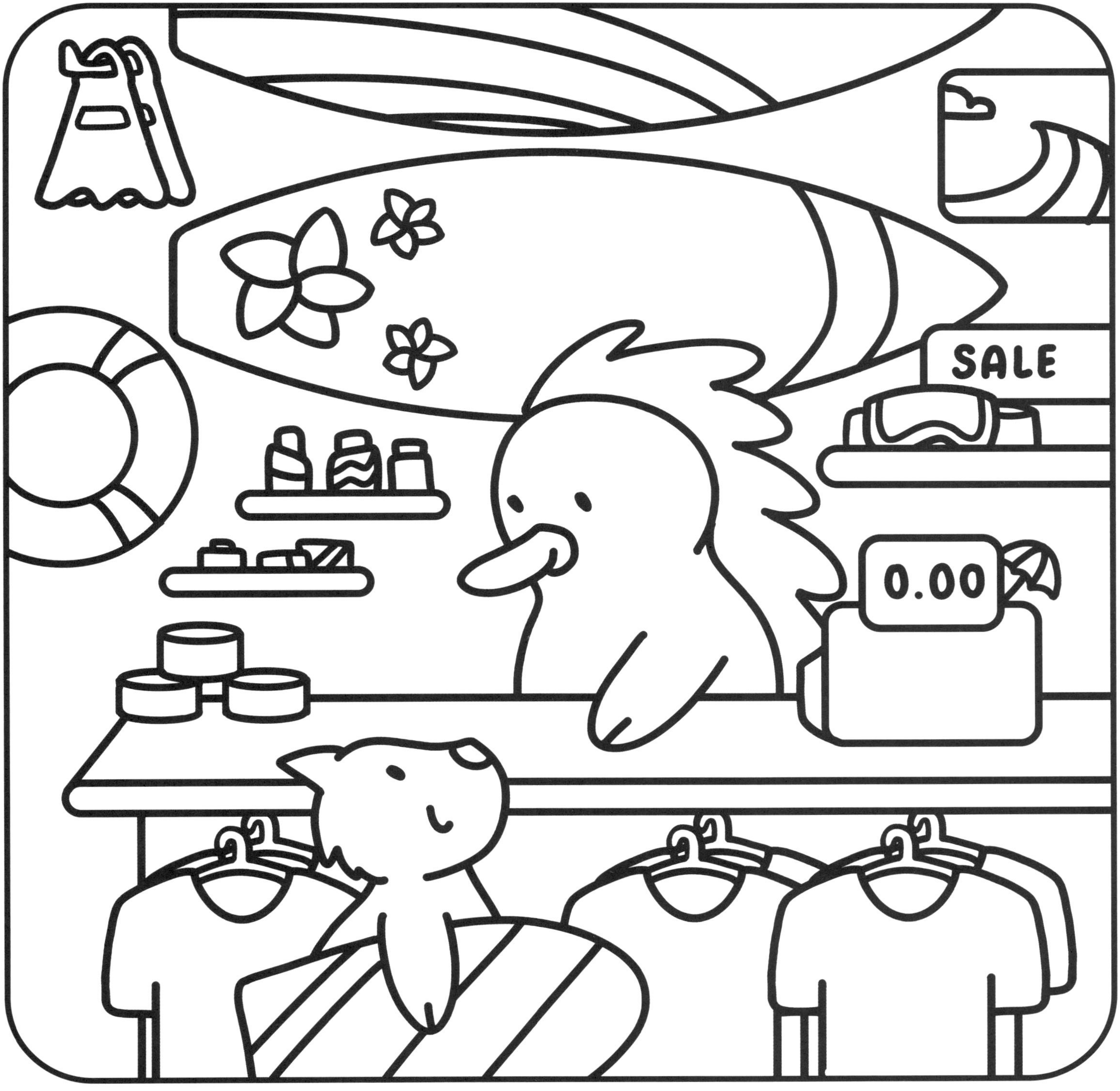
SALE
0.00

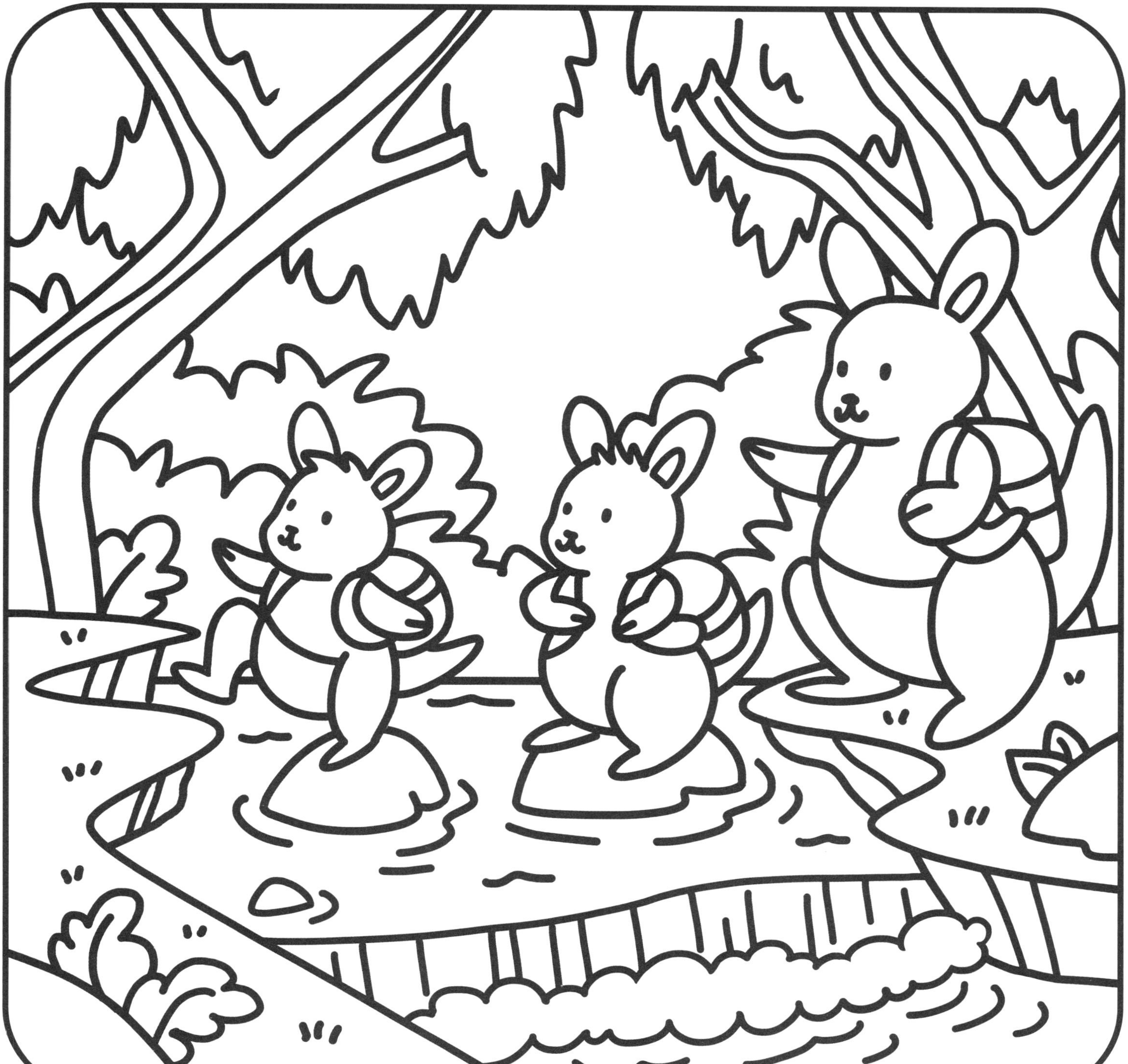

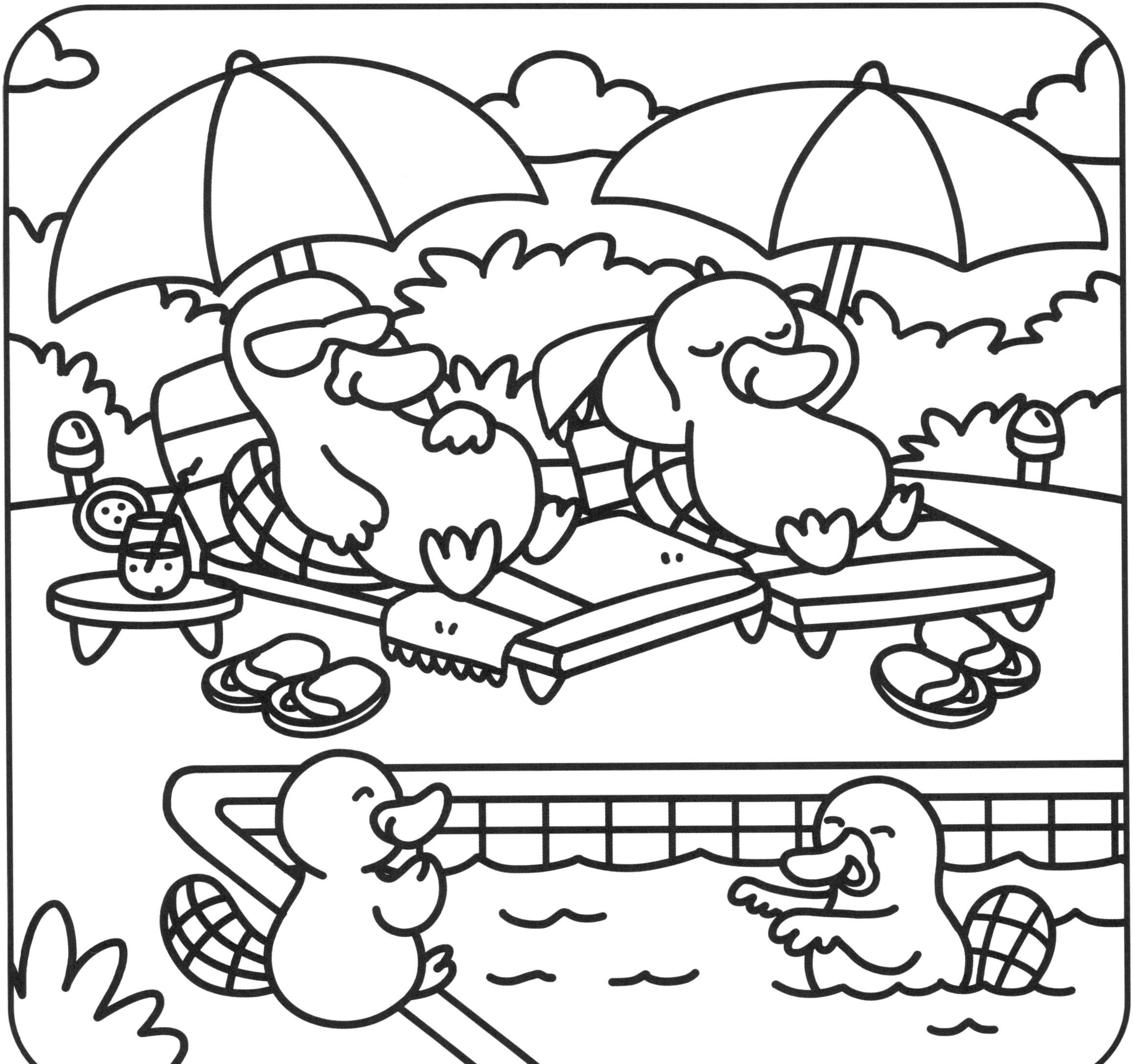

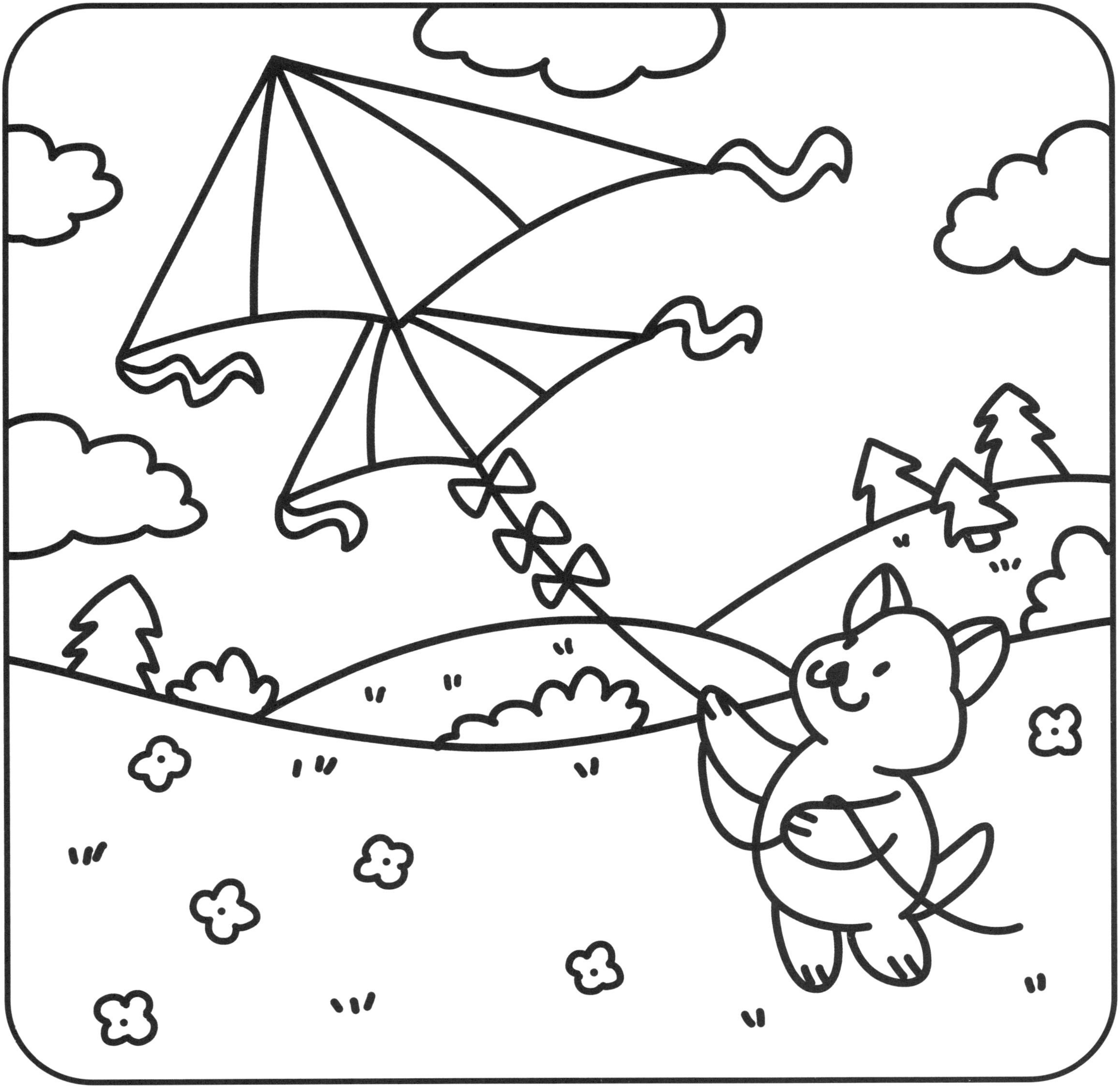

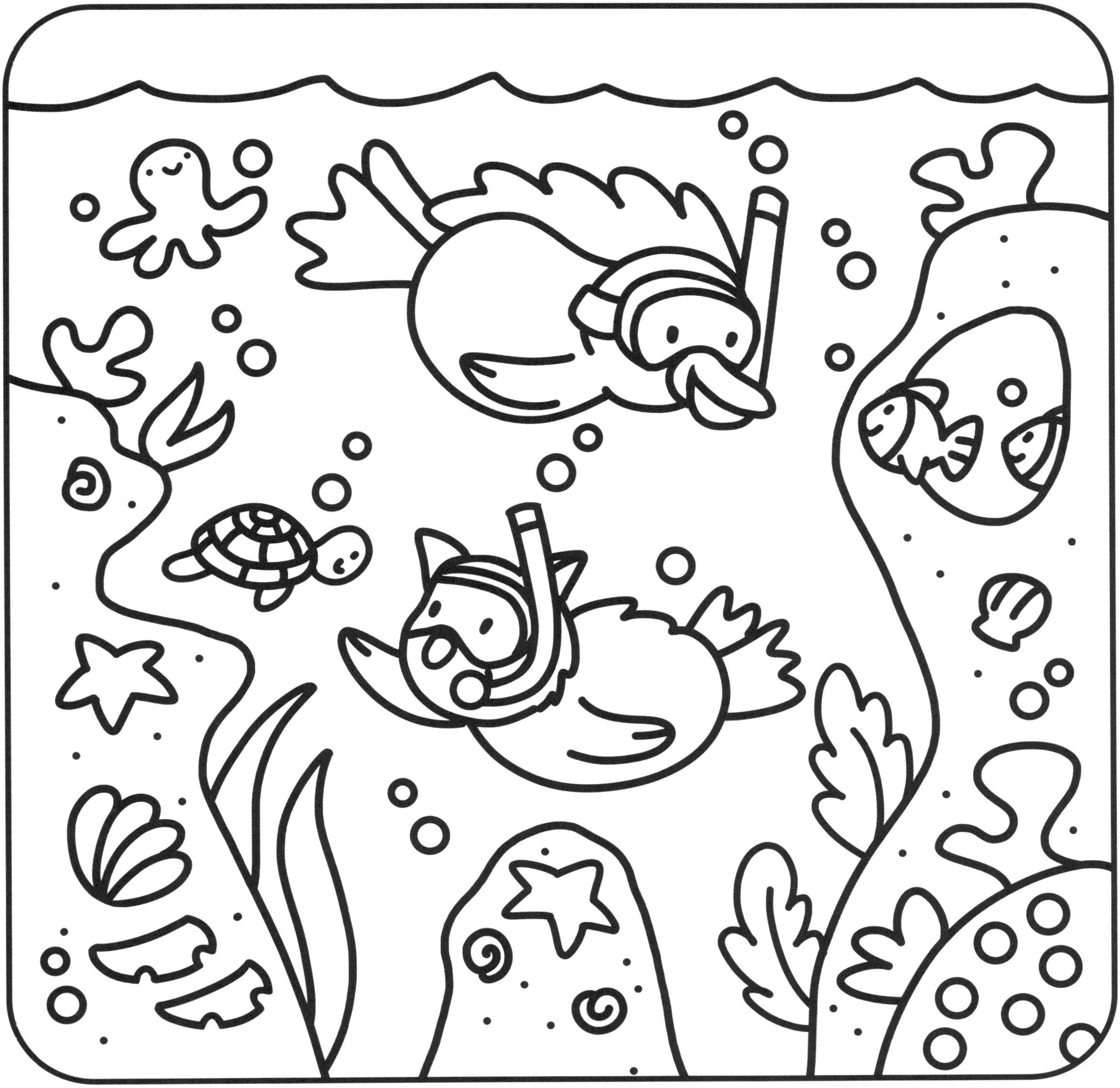

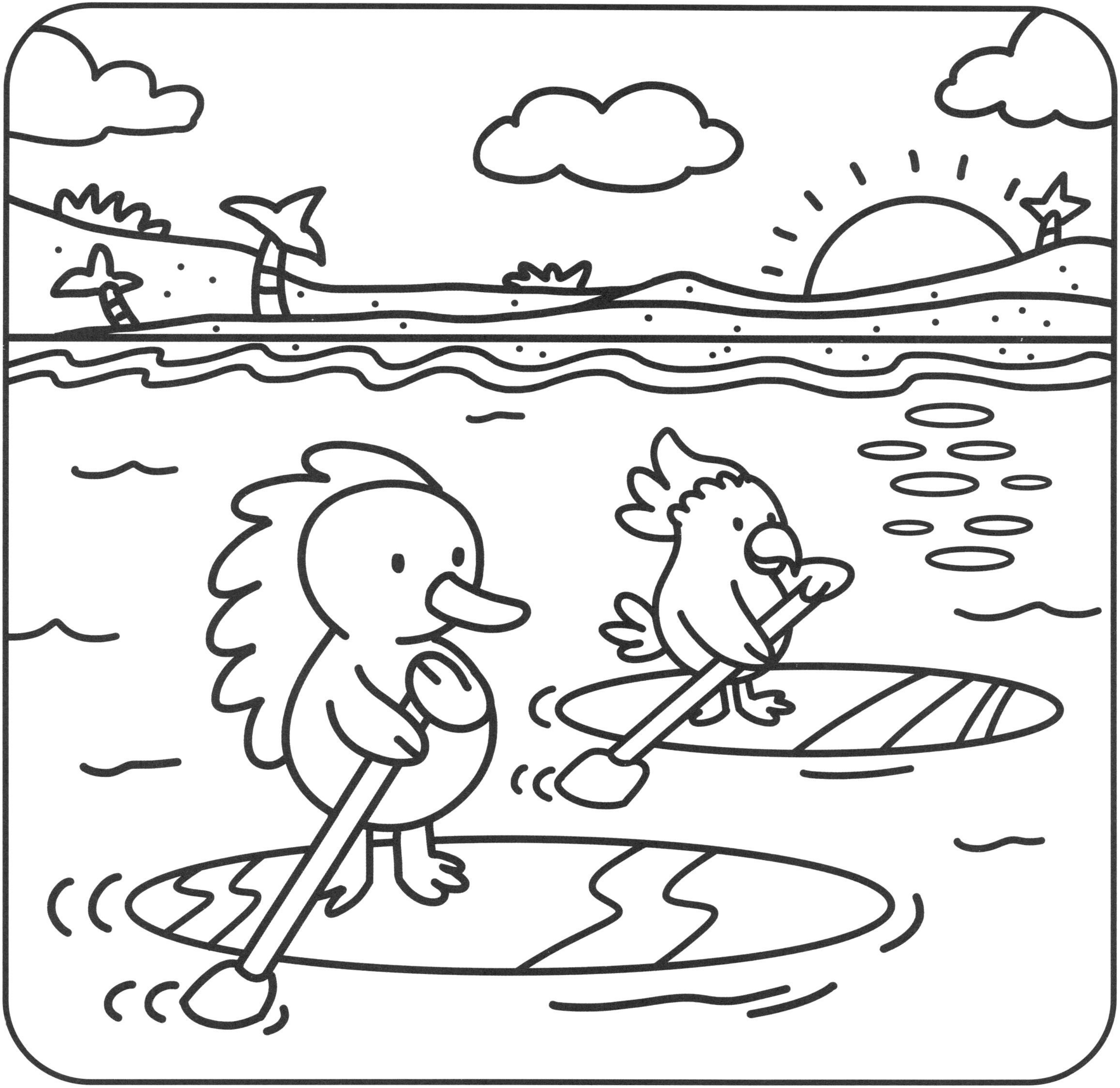

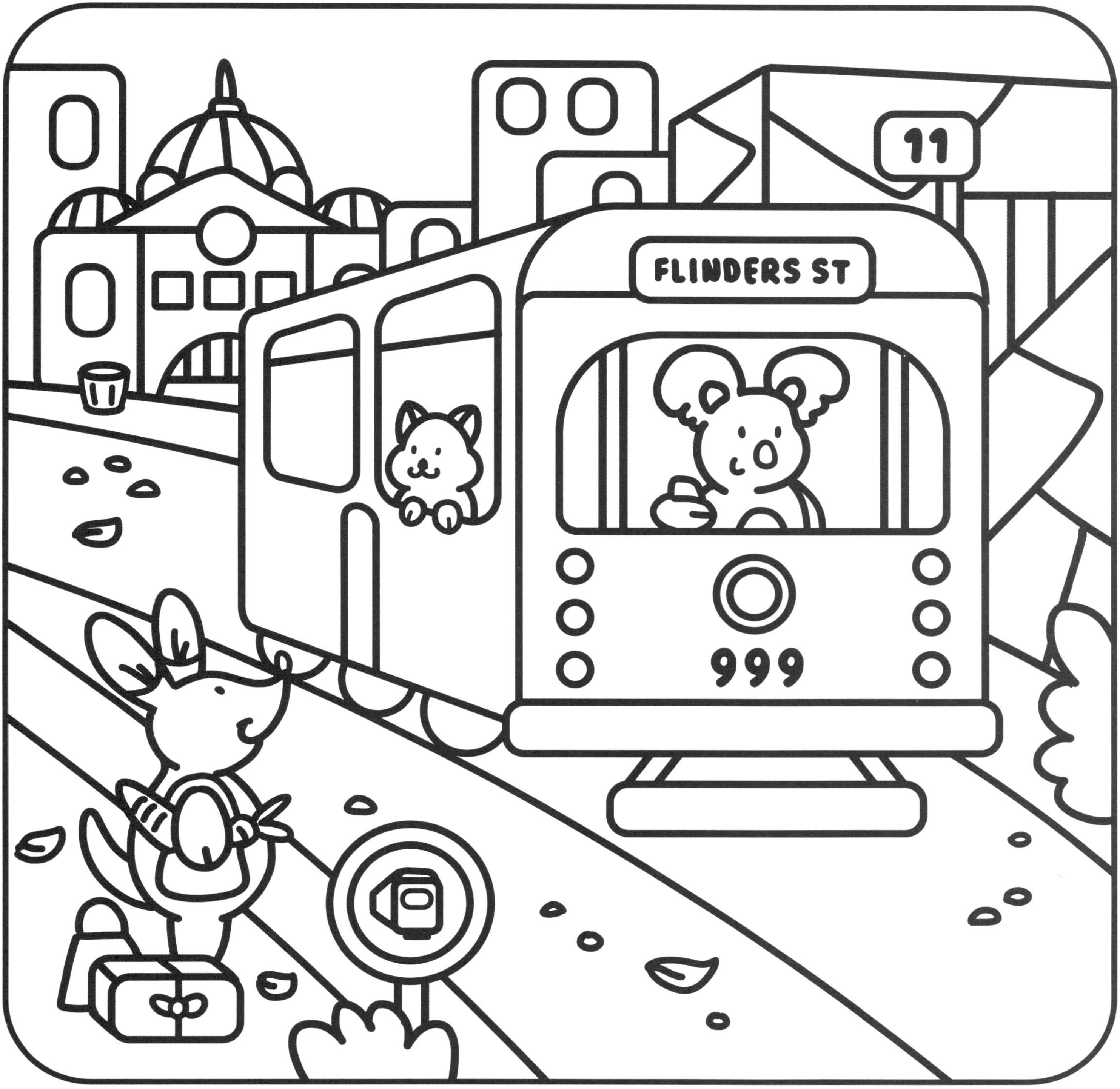
11
FLINDERS ST
999

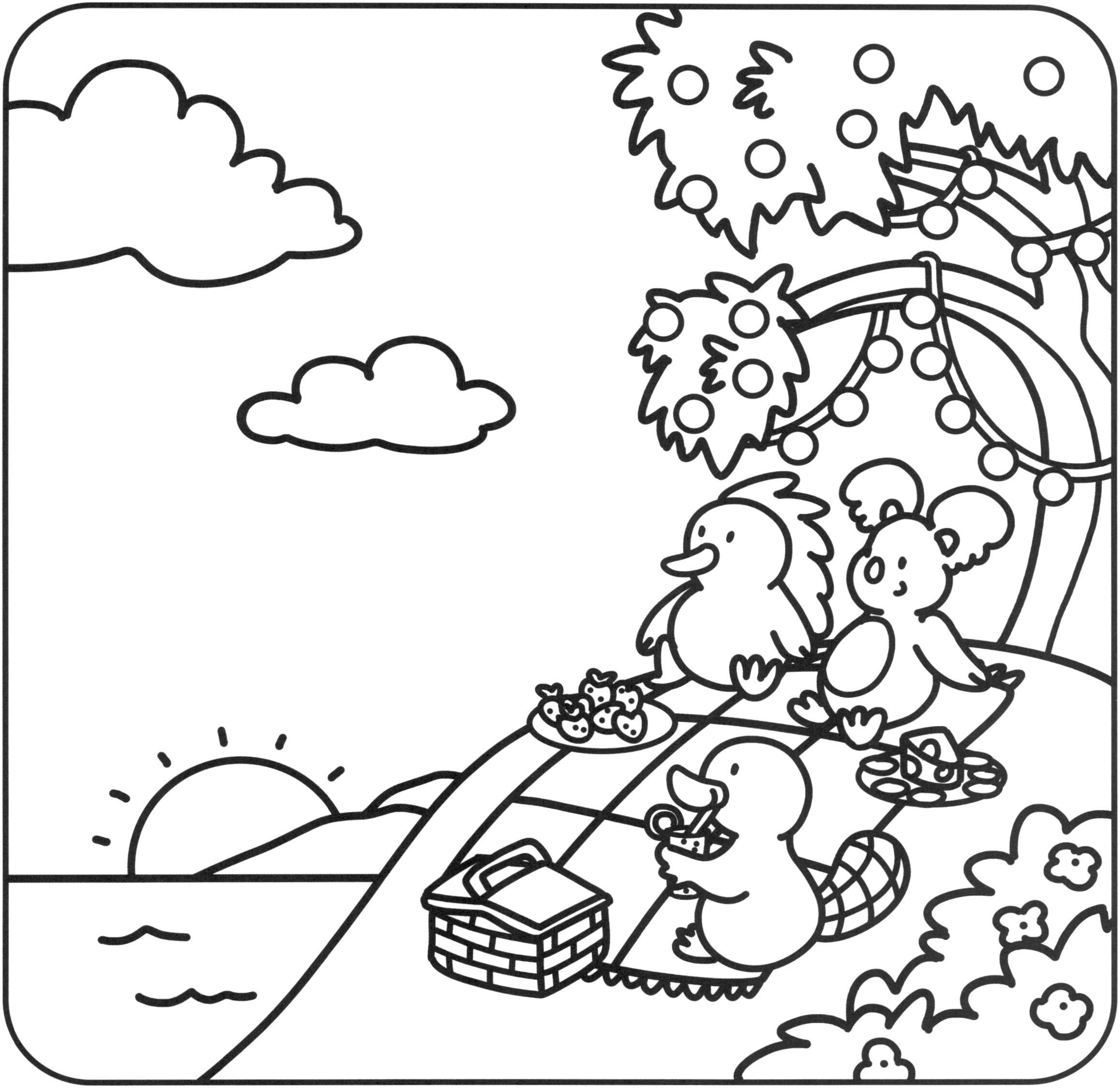

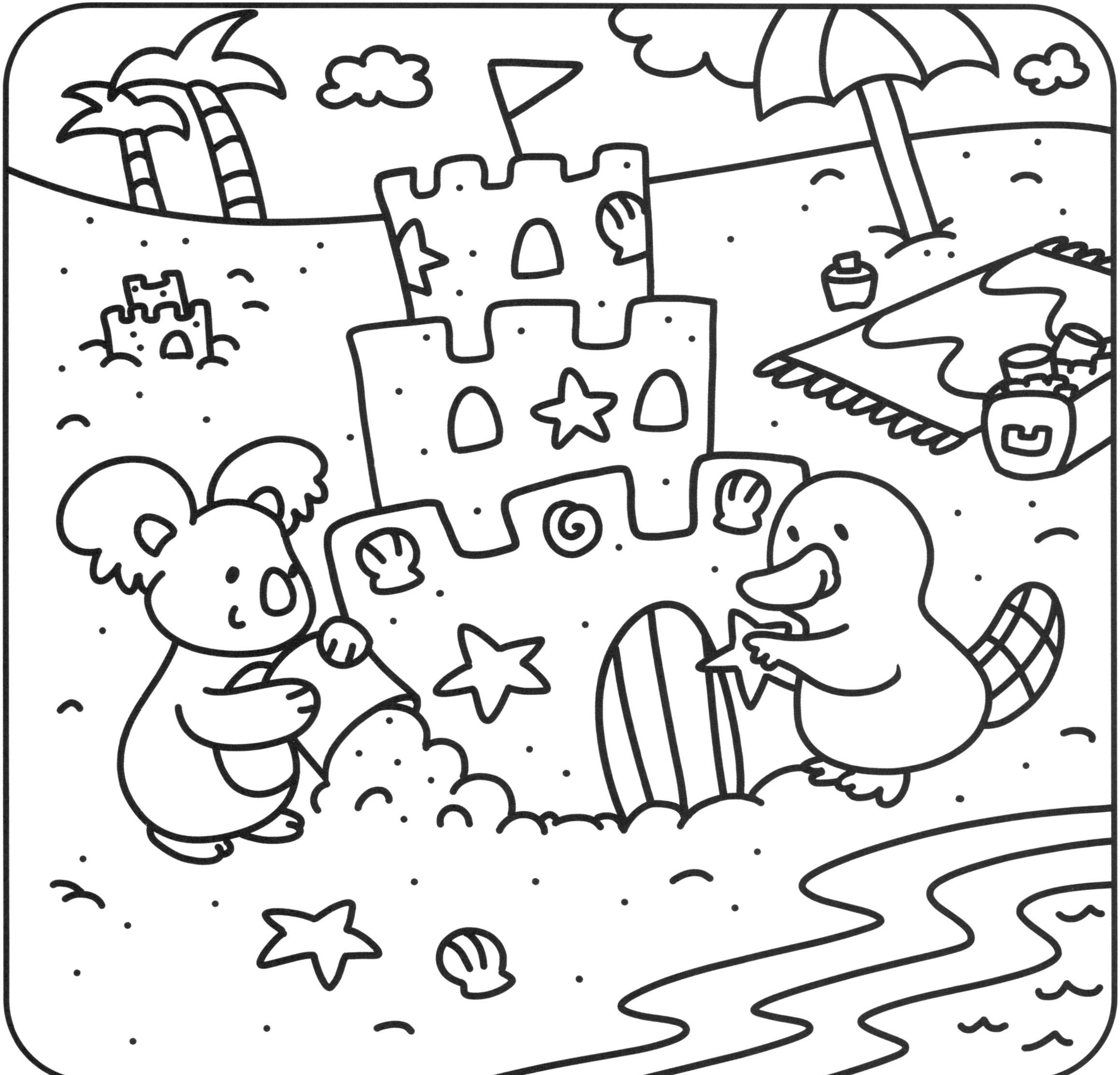

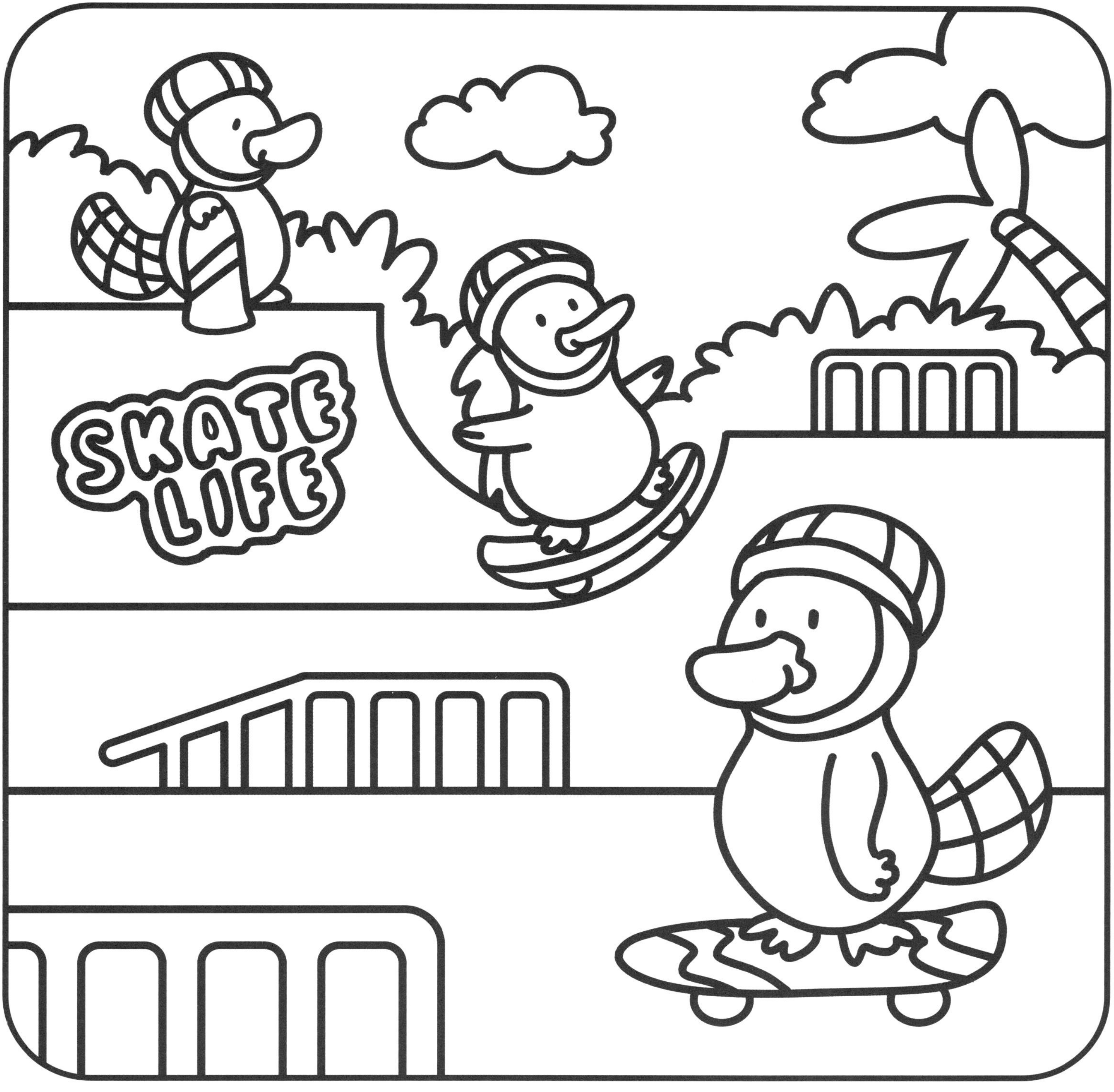
SKATE
LIFE

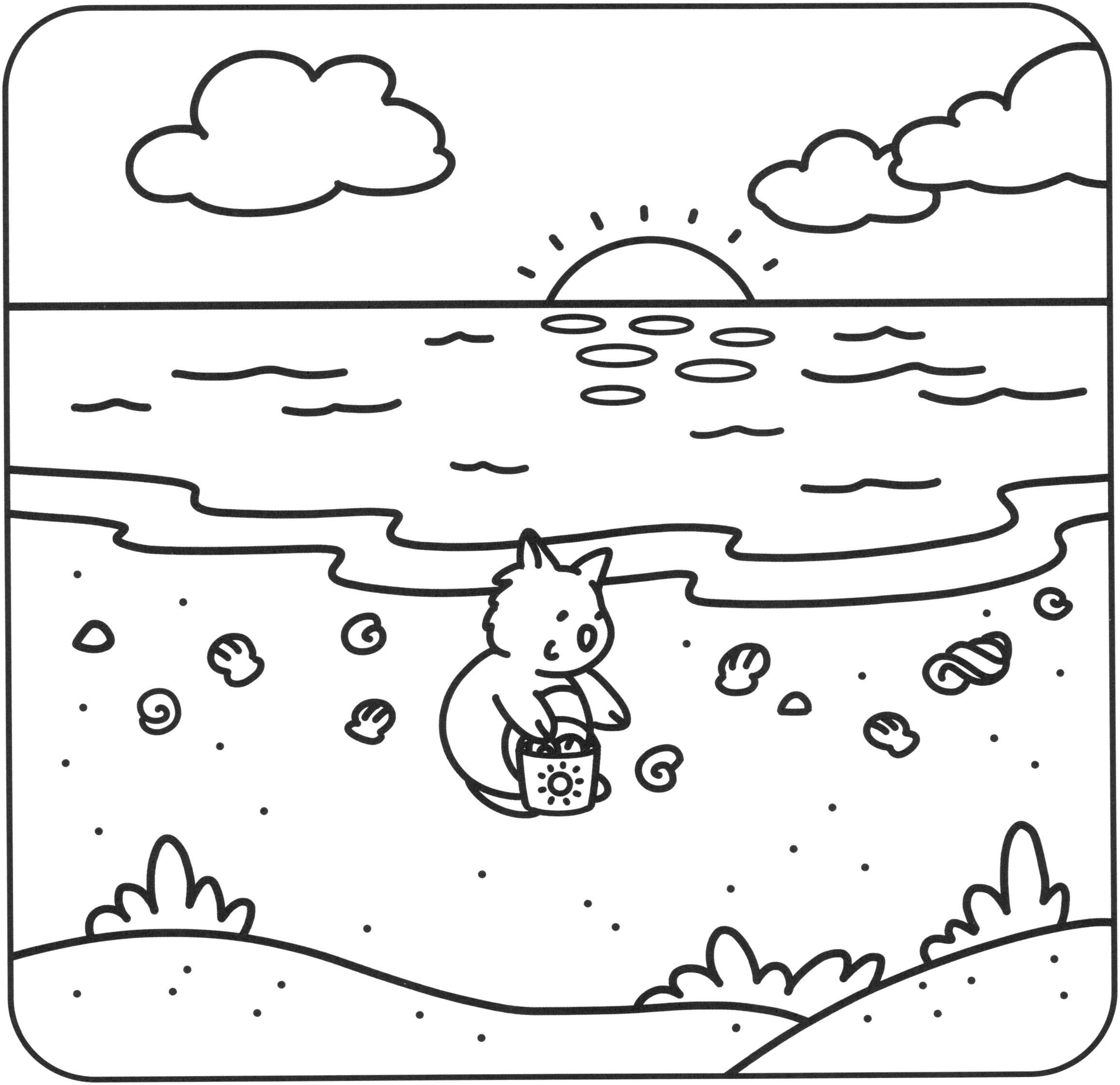

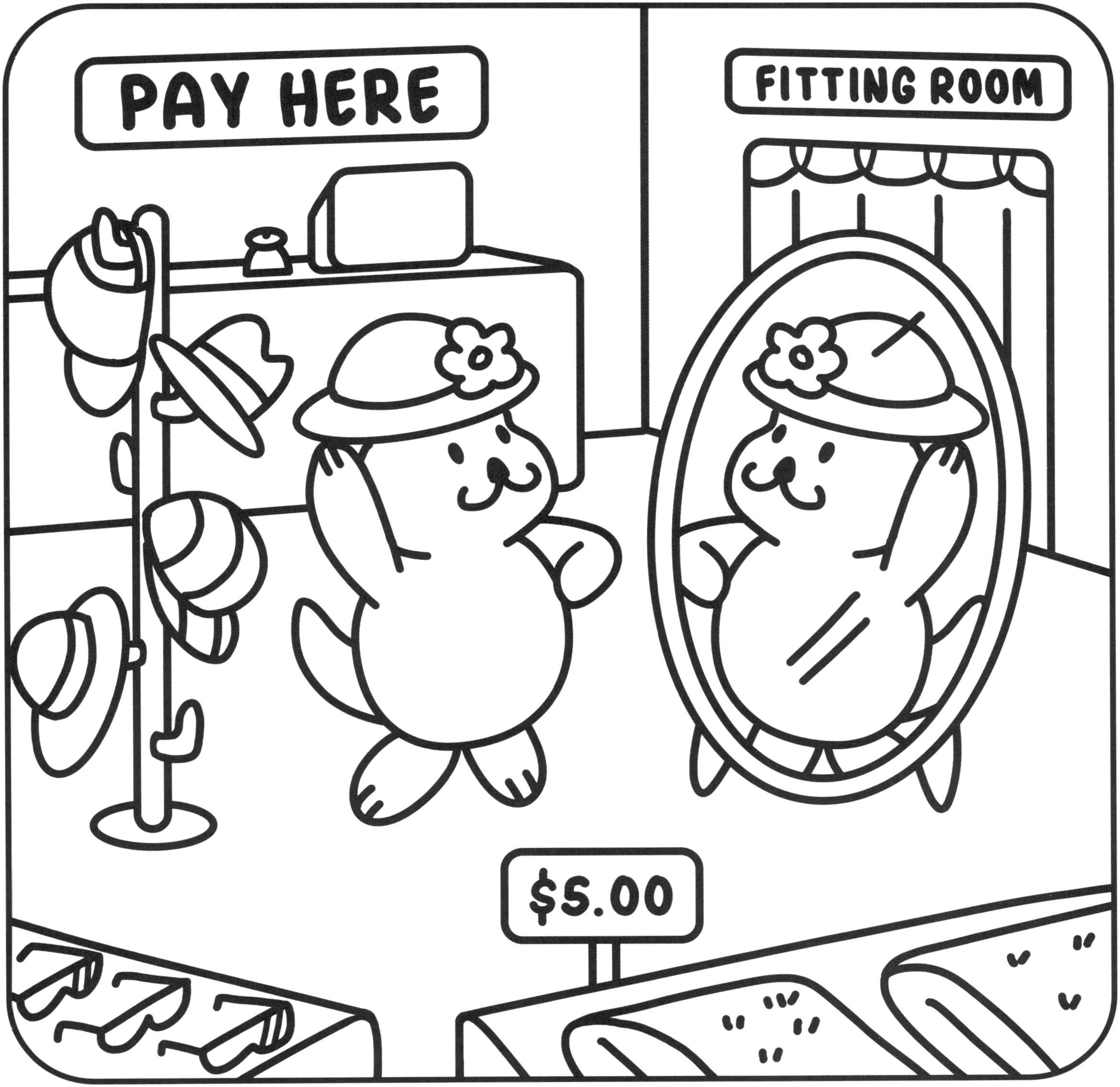
PAY HERE
FITTING ROOM
$5.00

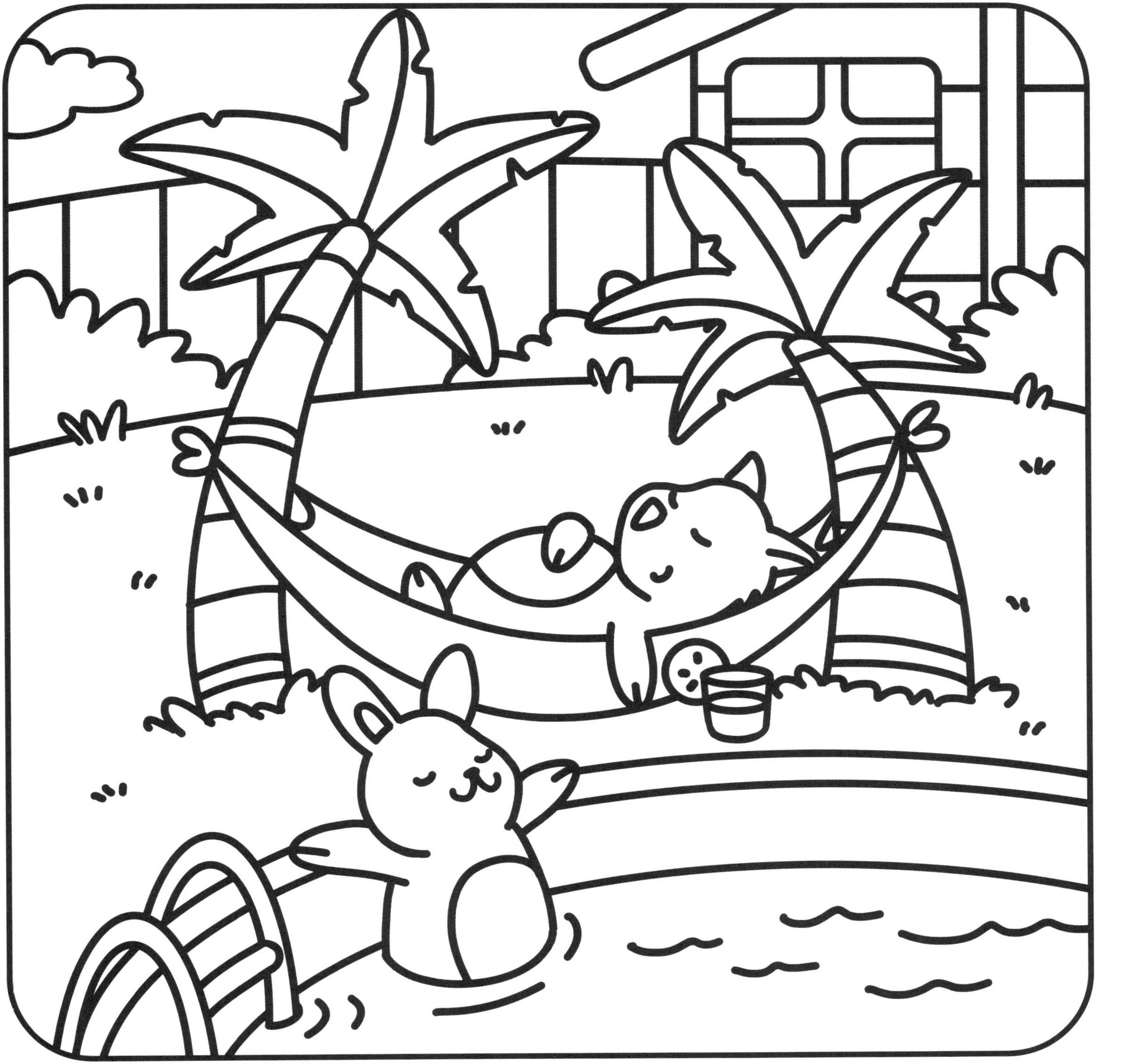

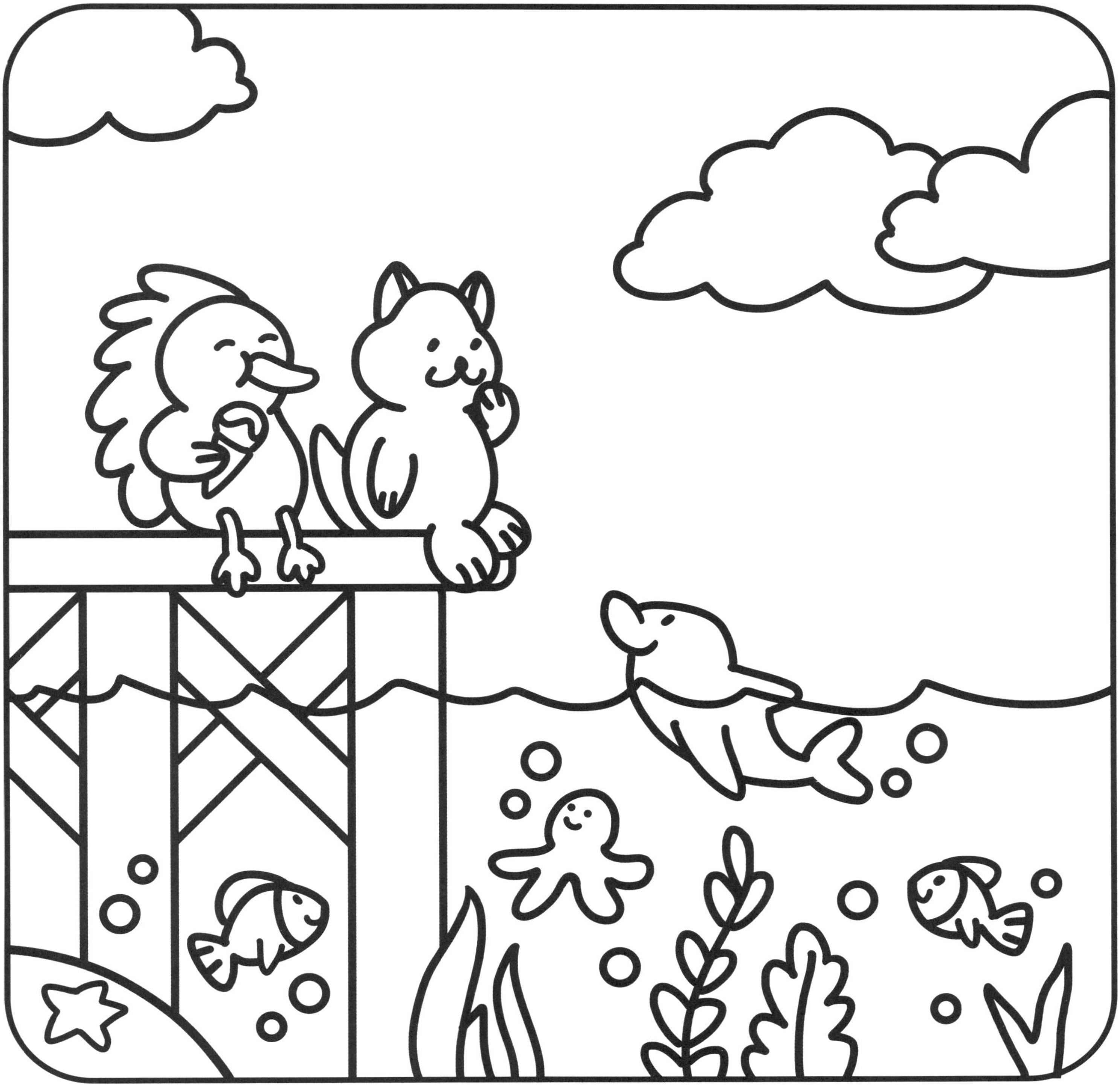

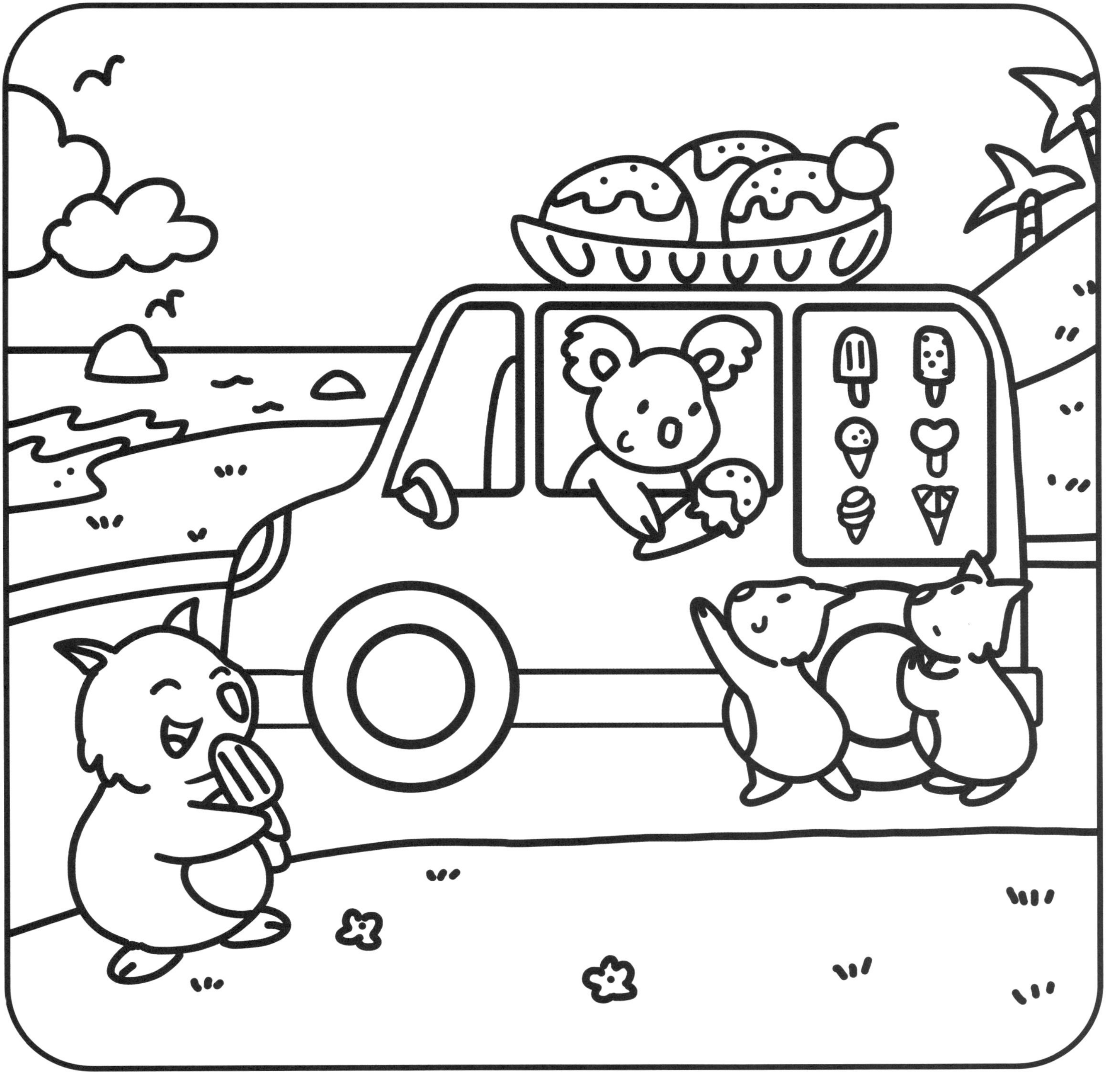

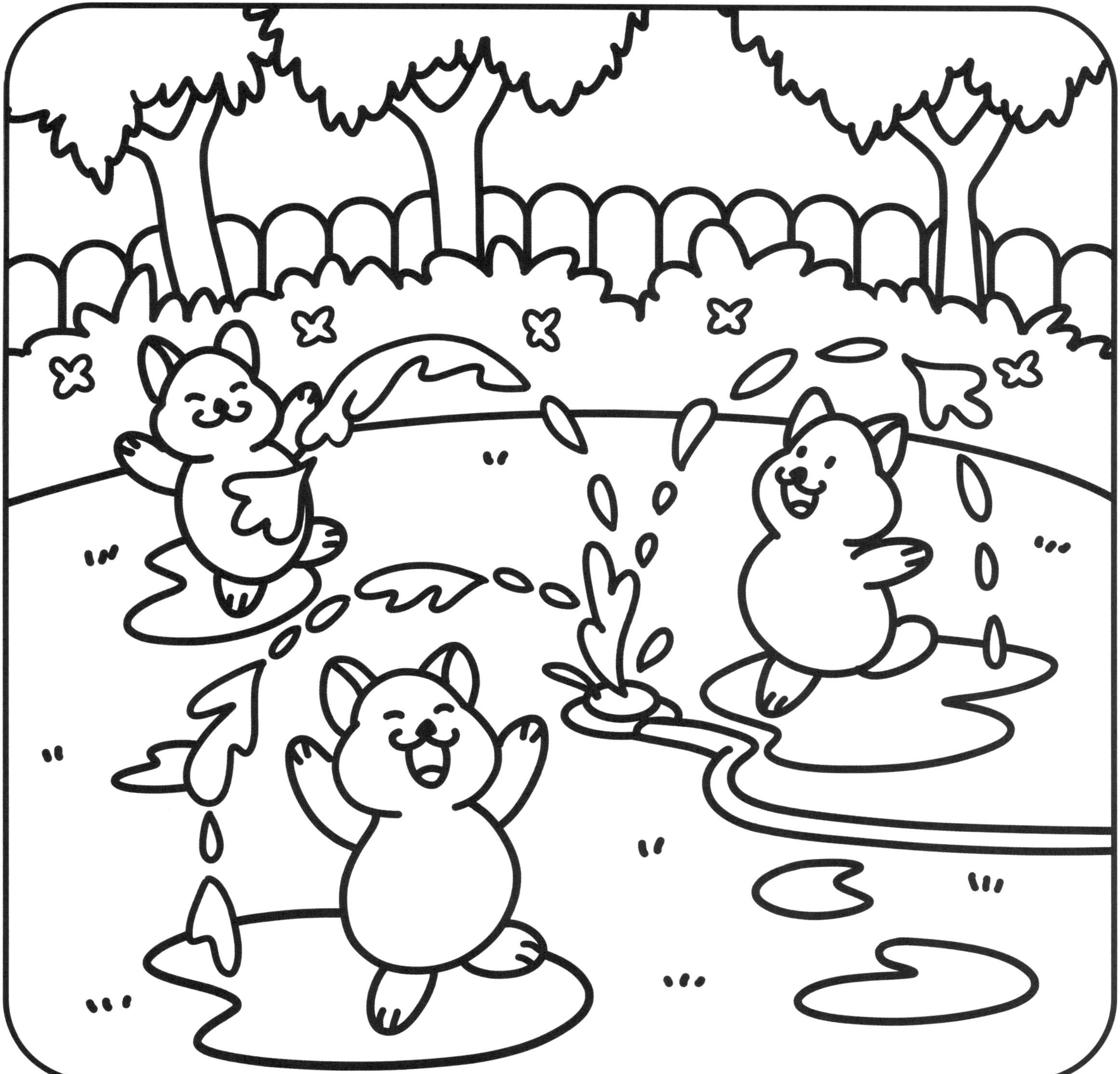

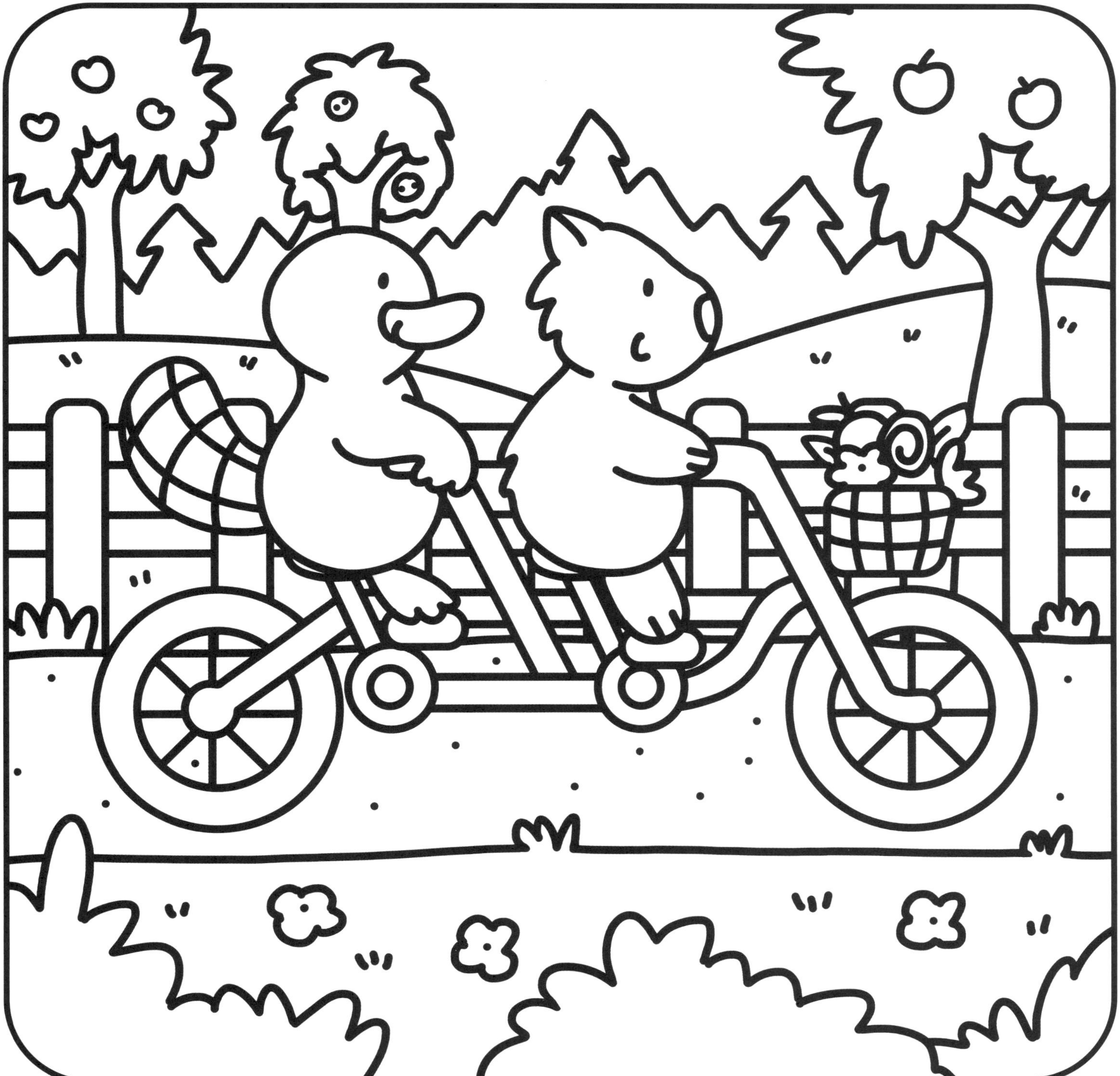

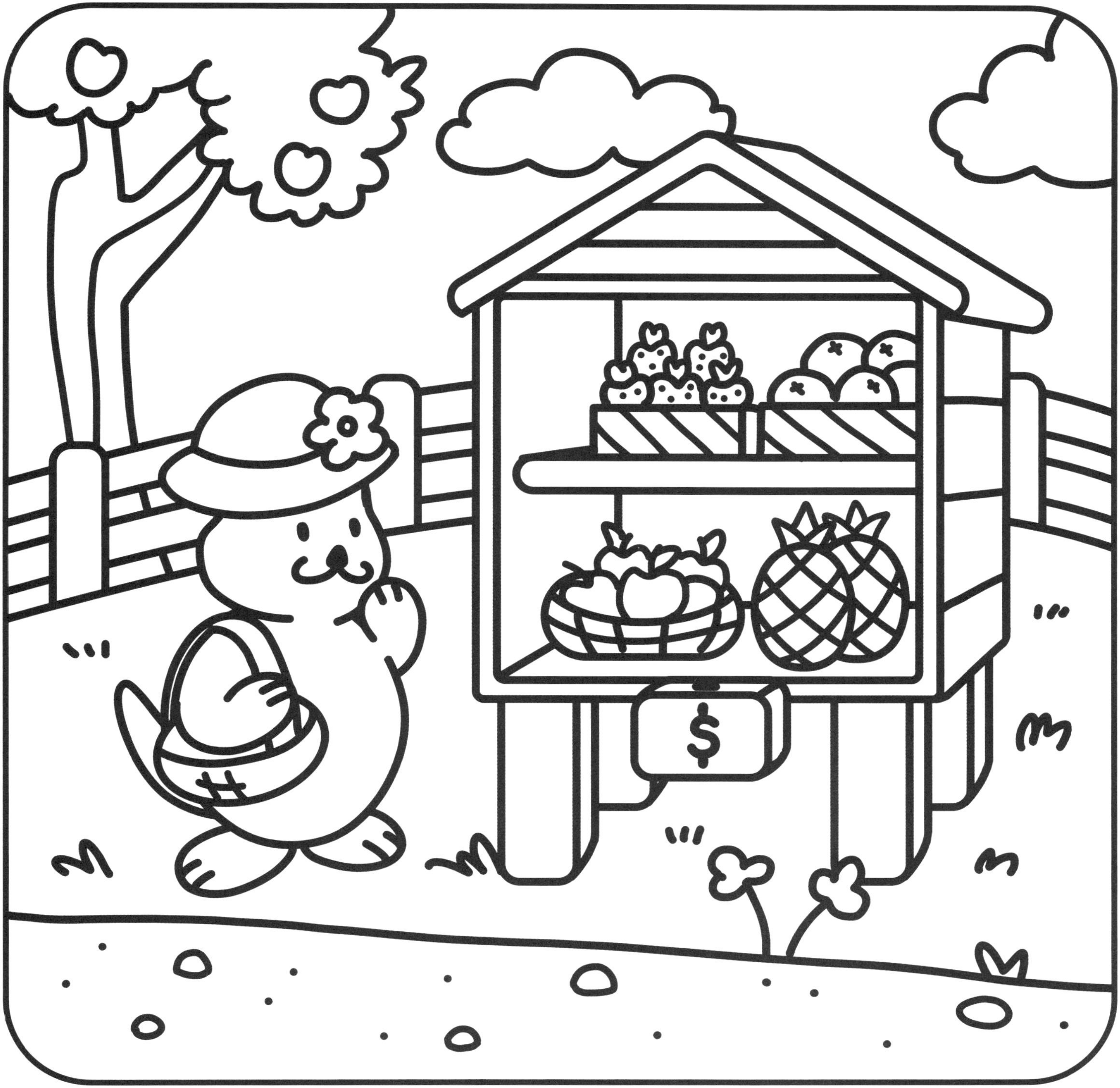

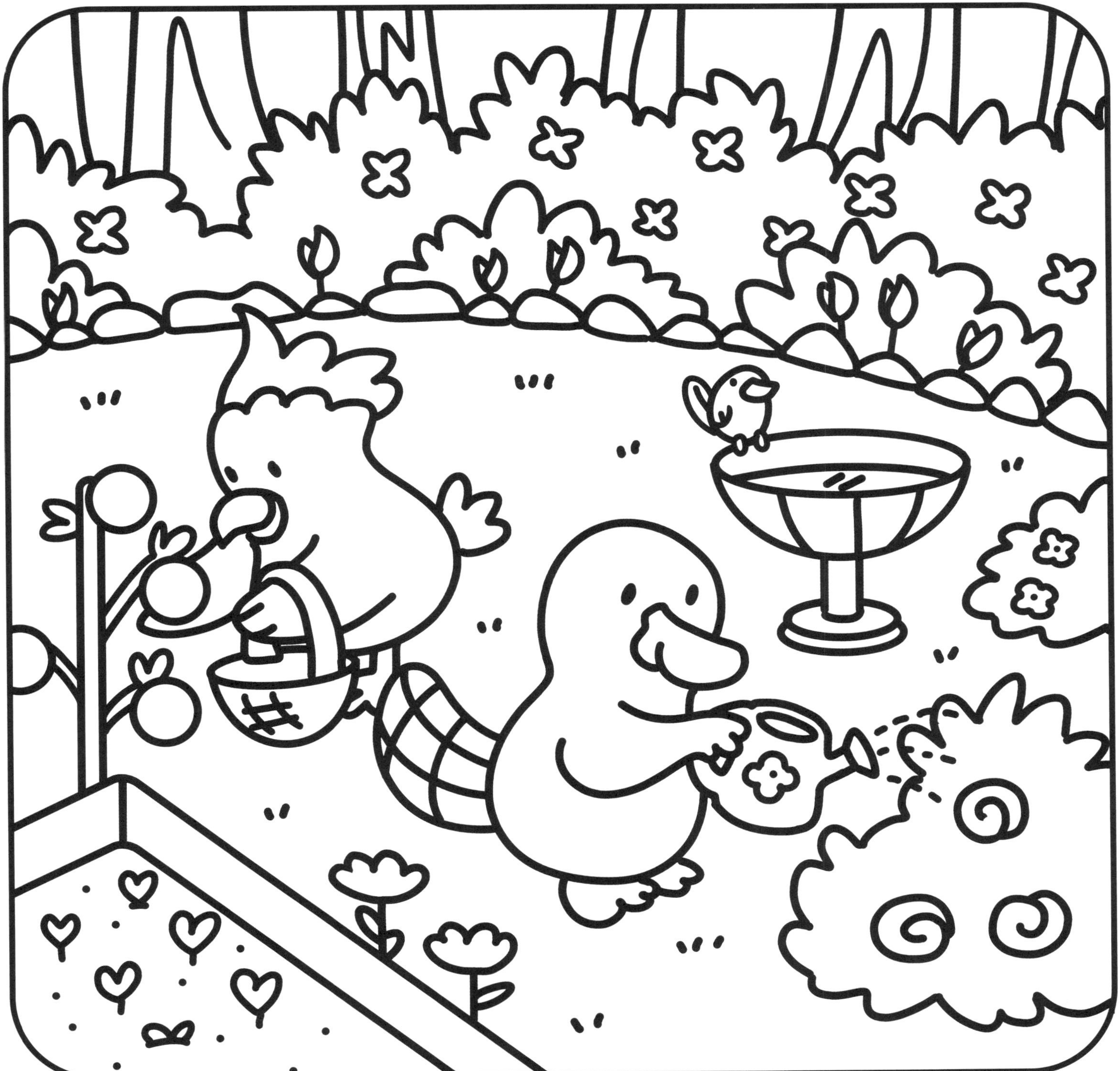

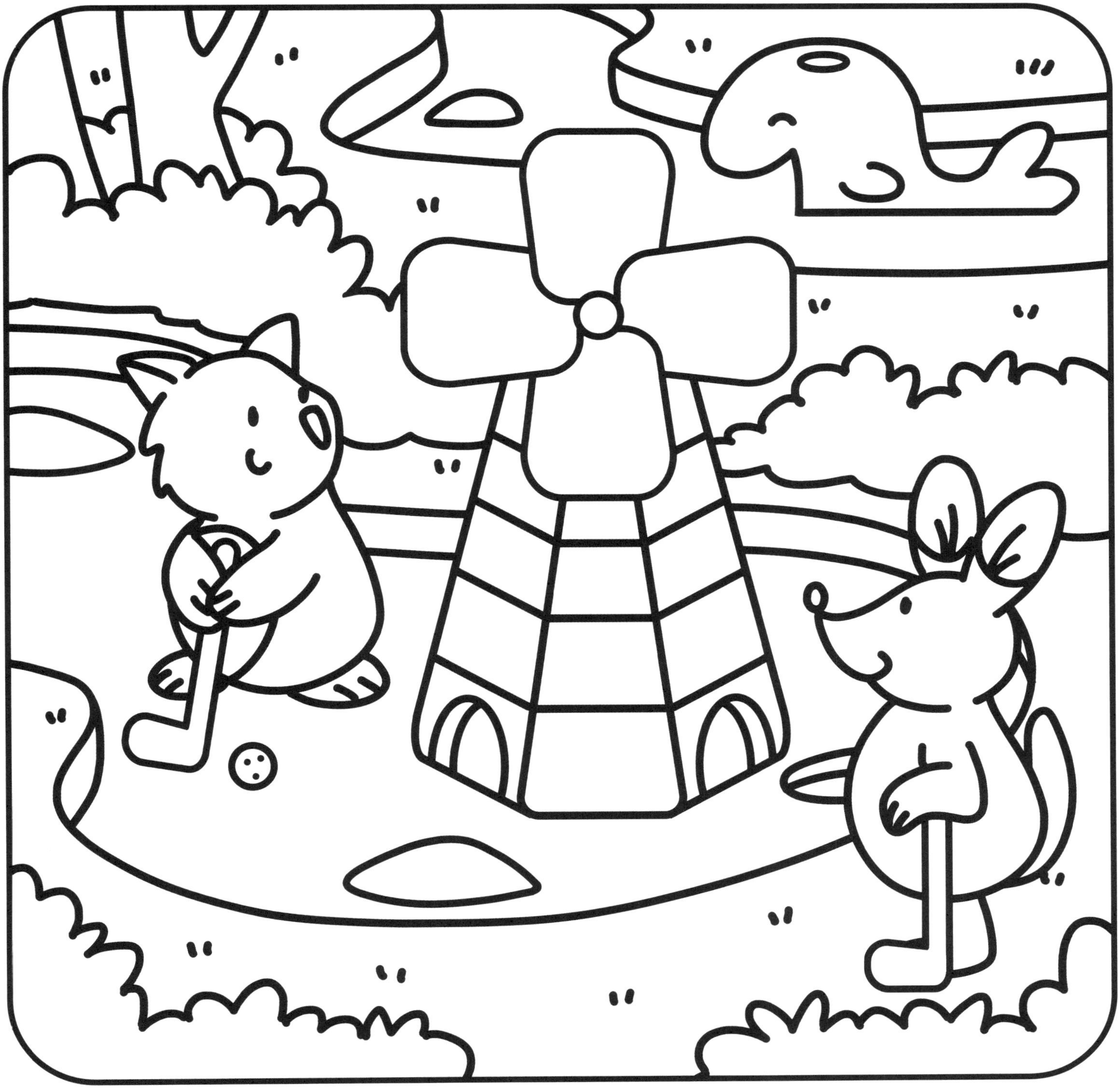

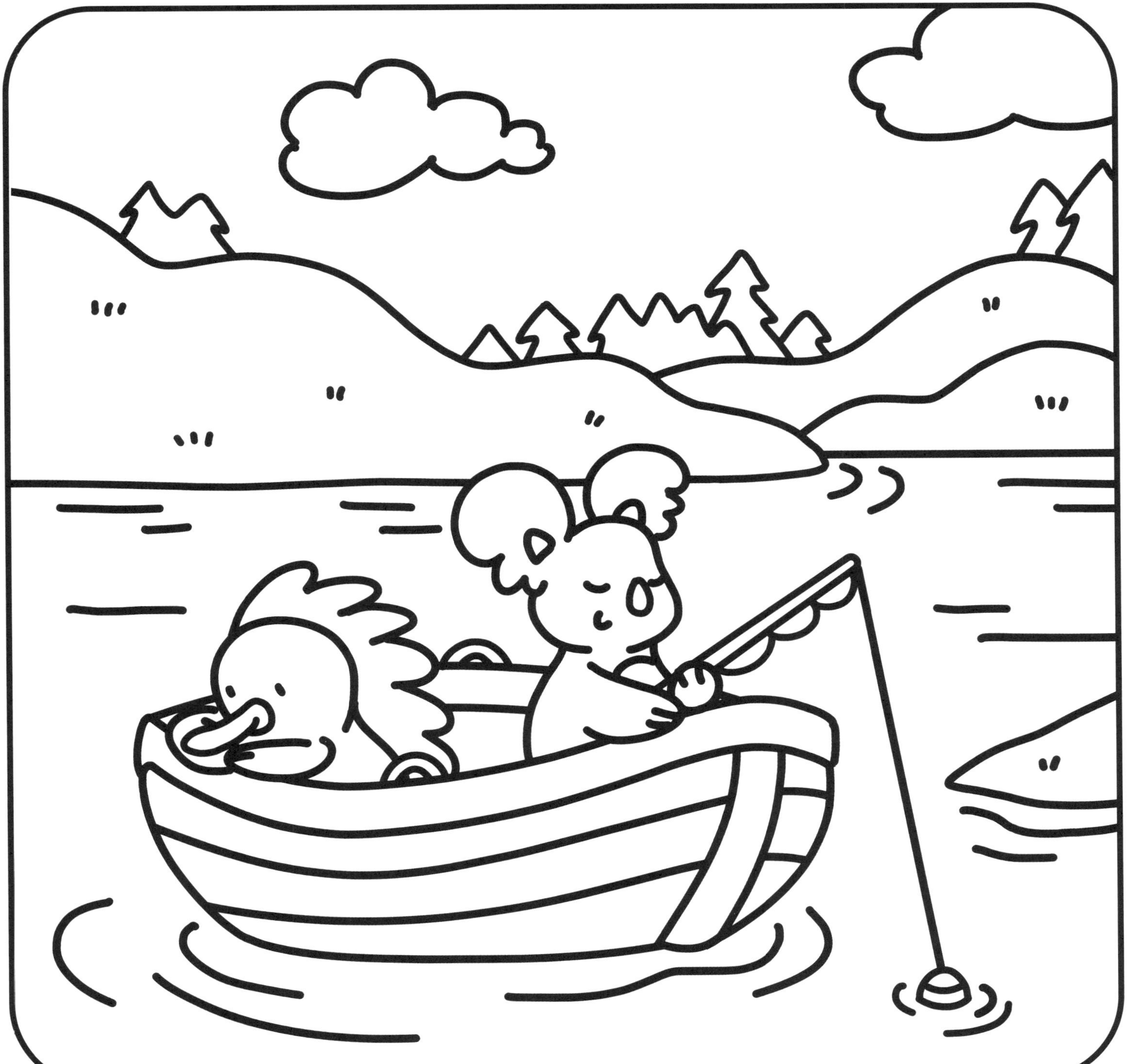

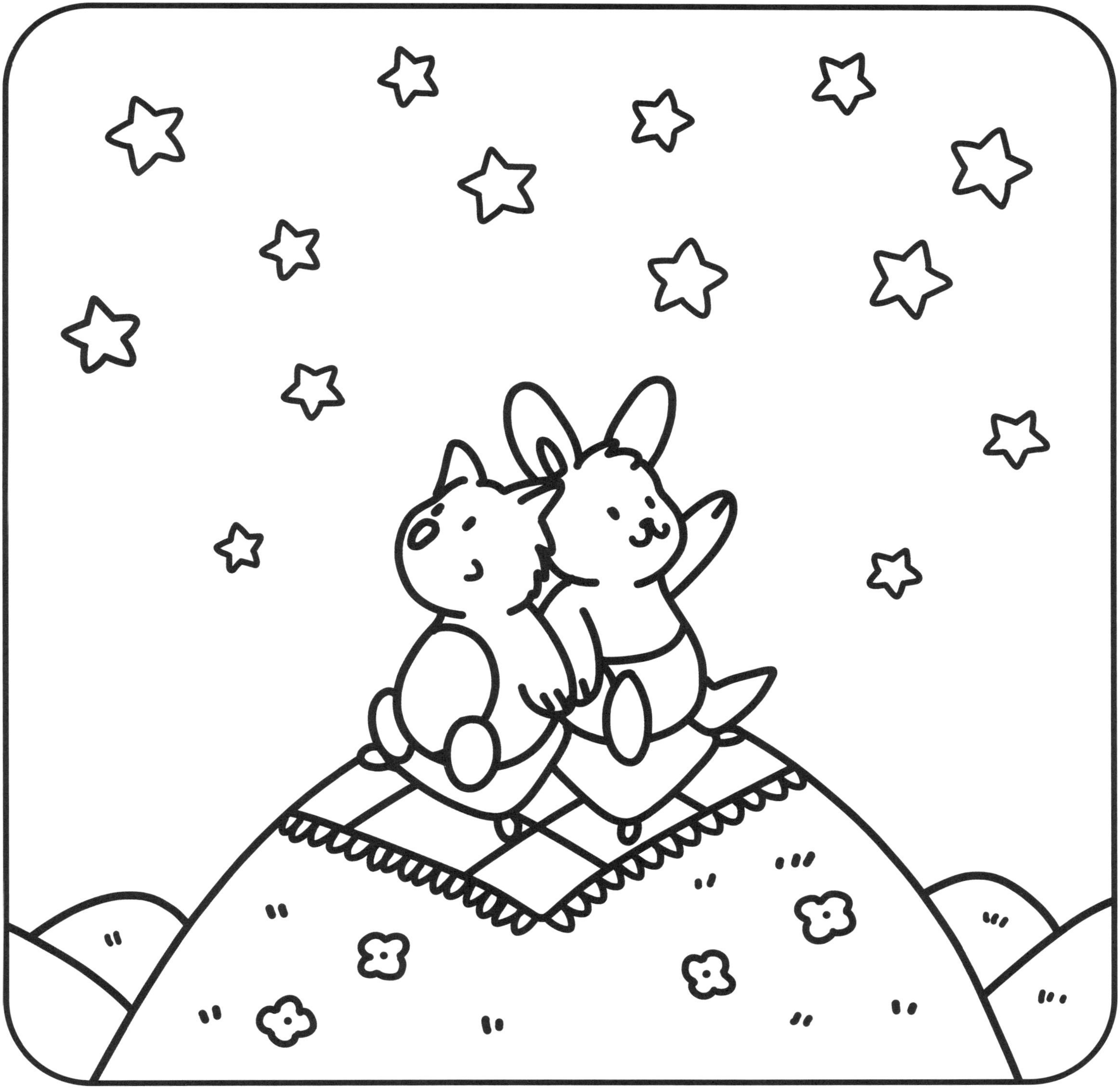